Wild Mammals
of
New England

FIELD GUIDE EDITION

Wild Mammals
of
New England

by
Alfred J. Godin

with drawings by the author

Field Guide edition adapted by
Harry Vanderweide

distributed by

The
Globe
Pequot
Press

Old Chester Road
Chester, Connecticut 06412

ISBN 0-89933-012-6

PUBLISHER'S NOTE

This field guide edition has been prepared from the full text of
WILD MAMMALS OF NEW ENGLAND by Alfred J.
Godin. This edition is published by arrangement with The
Johns Hopkins University Press and with the permission of
Alfred J. Godin.

Contents

Contents

Foreword

THE FIELD GUIDE EDITON OF WILD MAMMALS OF NEW ENGLAND is based on the full-length edition published by Johns Hopkins University Press, the most comprehensive work on the classification, distribution, ecology and behavior of wild mammals of New England states and their offshore waters ever published. The field guide edition has been condensed to eliminate technical source information while retaining the extensive data gathered for the original volume. It has also been rewritten with thought to eliminating most of the technical language so that it will be easily understood by anyone interested in learning about New England's mammals.

The research work that went into the volume was exhaustive. A biologist with the U.S. Fish and Wildlife Service, Alfred J. Godin, researched over a thousand scientific publications to prepare his original manuscript. In addition, he consulted with many biologists to update and correct the information. Godin personally examined over 20,500 specimens of New England wild mammals, and the pencil sketches that illustrate this book were drawn from his observations.

Without question, this field guide edition is the most complete volume on New England's wildlife that is popularly available to the general public, and it should prove a major contribution to understanding of these wonderful animals.

Harry Vanderweide, Editor
Augusta, Maine

Introduction

M AMMALS are the only animals with backbones in which the females have mammary glands producing milk to feed their young. The word mammal is derived from the Latin *mamma*, meaning "breast." Except for the duckbill platypus and the spiny anteaters, which lay eggs, mammals bear live young.

Mammals have hair at some stage of their development. Usually there are two types of hair; soft, thin underhair that grows thickly and provides warmth, and long, stiff outer hairs, called guard hairs which protect the underhair from wear. Whales, dolphins and porpoises are nearly hairless.

Mammals are warm-blooded, maintaining a constant body temperature regardless of environmental conditions. Some mammals hibernate—go into a deep, lethargic sleep—for weeks or even months, during which time their body temperature may be only slightly warmer than the surrounding air.

Except for the duckbill platypus, spiny anteaters, anteaters, pangolins and baleen whales, all adult mammals have teeth.

In the terminology of scientific classification, the mammals make up the class *Mammalia*, which is divided into orders (such as *Marsupalia*, animals with pouches, and *Carnivora*, meateaters). Each order is in turn divided into families (such as, within Carnivora, the Canidae family, coyotes, wolves and foxes, and Ursidae, bears) on the basis of shared characteristics. Families are divided into genera, and genera into species. The Latin species name (given in this book after the common name) defines each animal specifically and separates it from all others.

1. Mammals with Pouches

MARSUPIALS are among the most remarkable mammals because they have remained unchanged for the past 50 million years while many other species have evolved greatly. Because of this lack of change marsupials are often called living fossils. Adding to their strangeness, marsupials give birth to tiny, underdeveloped young and the female carries them in a pouch located on her abdomen where they nurse and grow. Included among marsupials are kangaroos, bandicoots, wallabies, and opossums. Some of these animals live in trees, others are surface runners and leapers, some make burrows and others spend much time in the water.

Marsupials are found in Australia west to Celebes and the Moluccas, in North, Central and South America, and have been introduced to New Zealand.

Opossums

Opossums are small to medium-sized animals with short legs. All 4 feet have 5 distinct toes. The big toe of the hind foot is clawless and opposable to the other toes for ease in climbing. Some opossums are omnivorous, taking both plant and animal matter, while others eat only animals or insects.

Opossums are found from Argentina north through Mexico, the eastern and central United States, and southeastern Canada (Ontario). They have also been introduced into several areas of the western United States.

Virginia Opossum
Didelphis virginiana

The Virginia opossum is the only member of its family found in New England. "Playing 'possum" has become part of the language to indicate someone pretending to be dead or knocked out. When the opossum is threatened it will often go into a coma-like state, becoming limp and lifeless, staying that way from a few minutes up to 6 hours.

Description: An adult opossum is about the size of a large house cat but has a heavier body and shorter legs. The head is cone-shaped with a pointed snout and sharp teeth. It has beady eyes and big, thin, naked, leathery ears. The tail is long, tapering, scantily haired and scaly. It is prehensile and the opossum can use it to hang from branches.

Adult female opossums have prominent pouches lined with soft fur. There are from 9 to 17 nipples inside the pouch, the usual number being 13, arranged in a horseshoe shape with 1 or 2 nipples in the center.

Opossums have rather long and coarse fur. The face has cat-like whiskers. The color of fur and skin vary widely depending on the region the animal is living in. In the north opossums have relatively thick underfur which is whitish at the base, sometimes tipped with black, and overlaid with a thin covering of pale guard hairs; this makes them look gray and grizzled. In the south, opossums tend to have less underfur and to be darker in color. The head is pale yellow to white except for a narrow black line

VIRGINIA OPOSSUM

down the center. The ears are black and usually edged with white. The belly appears more grizzled or darker than the back, where white guard hairs are more abundant. The legs are dark brown or black, as are the feet with the toes partly white. The tail is black at the base and becomes flesh-colored in its last two-thirds. Males and females look alike, as do the young, and they don't change appearance with the changing seasons. All-white, albino and cinnamon-colored opossums occur, but rarely. Opossums do shed their fur, but it takes place slowly, a few hairs at a time.

Male opossums are larger than females. Adults range from 24 to 32 inches long with tails from 9 to 13 inches long, and hind feet from 2 to 3 inches long. They weigh from 4 to 12 pounds.

Distribution: Opossums are found throughout the wooded areas of the eastern United States and southeastern Canada, south to Middle America. Within the past century they have expanded their range north and west. They were not found in New England before 1900. They are now found throughout Connecticut, Rhode Island and Massachusetts, except the offshore islands, and are found in southern Vermont, New Hampshire, and extreme southern Maine.

Ecology: Opossums live in a wide variety of habitats, from wet to dry, but are most common near streams and swamps. Since they aren't good at digging they use the abandoned burrows and dens of other animals, tree cavities, hollow logs, rock piles, brush, wood and trash piles, spaces beneath buildings and drainpipes. They seldom stay in the same place 2 nights in a row.

Man, dogs, foxes, bobcats, hawks and great horned owls prey on opossums, and many of the slow-moving animals are killed by automobiles. Opossums are bothered by fleas and ticks and infested by a variety of internal parasites. They are thought to be highly resistant to rabies infection.

Behavior: The opossum has a head about the size of a raccoon's, but the raccoon has a brain 5 times larger. The small and primitive structure of the opossum's brain helps explain its slow-witted behavior, but despite this handicap the opossum has expanded its North American range over a wide area in a surprisingly small amount of time.

Opossums are not social animals, and a meeting of two adults is likely to result in a fight. They are nocturnal, or night animals. They begin to move about at dusk and keep going until dawn. In the fall and winter, opossums become less active the colder it gets, although they do not hibernate.

They like to climb, and take to trees to escape enemies or find fruit. Opossums climb hand over hand, using the tail for balance, and typically appear slow and clumsy. They usually climb down head first. On the ground they have a slow, ambling gait, with the tail swinging in pronounced sideways and up-and-down motions. They walk at less than a mile an hour and hit about 4½ miles an hour at a dead run.

A walking opossum will often sniff the air and will sometimes stand on its hind feet for a second or 2 to look around. Opossums have sharp senses of touch and smell, but their hearing is not keen and they seem to be nearsighted.

An opossum will rarely turn on a pursuer and usually will try to reach trees or some other protective cover. If caught in the open, an opossum will crouch down, hiss, growl and screech. Even more often it will simply "play 'possum," flopping over as though dead, usually leaving the mouth open with the cheeks drawn back, showing teeth as though in a cynical grin. Sometimes the tongue will stick out a little. Often such a catatonic opossum will drool and breath shallowly.

When an opossum is grabbed it has even more defenses. It will defecate, pass gas and give off a foul-smelling greenish fluid from two small paps near the anus.

Usually opossums don't make any noise, but when they are angry they hiss or make a clicking sound with their teeth showing and they give a low growl. They are usually clean animals;

caged opossums have been seen licking their paws and faces like a cat to clean their fur after eating.

The opossum is confident in the water and a good, although slow, swimmer. When threatened in the water the opossum will dive and swim at least 20 feet underwater with its eyes open. It can travel 100 yards underwater with ease.

The size of the area an opossum uses for its home range varies considerably from animal to animal, but around half a mile might be a good average. In fall and winter the opossum works twice as long at feeding and taking care of its nest compared to the rest of the year. While it has been spreading its territory north, the opossum is not well-equipped to face cold weather. While it will have a good layer of fat larded on by winter, the opossum's fur doesn't provide much real protection from the cold. On the worst winter days the opossum usually stays in its den, but if it gets really hungry it will go out—even if the temperature is below zero. When this happens the opossum suffers heavy frostbite to the ears and tail, and those living in the north often are missing the tips of their ears or tails.

Opossums lap water like a dog, taking 7 to 17 ounces of water in 24 hours. True opportunists, opossums eat almost anything, including carrion.

The mating season extends from January or February into June or July. Once bred, the female wants no more to do with the male and will fight him off if he continues to make advances. In New England opossums have 2 or 3 litters a year.

The birth of baby opossums occurs about 13 days after breeding. The mother licks the newborn as they emerge transparent and the size of honeybees, and they crawl upward with a swimming motion into the pouch where each attaches to a nipple. The average litter is 8 but gets as high as 21. The young stay attached inside the pouch for 50 to 65 days, growing fast. They are weaned 95 to 105 days after birth. When 2 months old their eyes open and they leave the pouch for short periods. Often young opossums will ride on their mother's back, clinging to her fur with feet and tails. They stay with their mother for about another month, returning to the pouch when necessary for milk or protection, before they begin to take care of themselves completely. Usually at least 2 weeks occur between the time one litter is weaned and the next is born.

Female opossums are sexually mature at 1 year old, and they can live to be at least 7 years old.

2. Insect Eaters

THE INSECT EATERS, or Insectivora, are the smallest of the true mammals. They usually have a long snout extending well beyond the mouth, beady eyes, and a slender head.

These are voracious animals which eat a great deal of food each day. While most of them feed mainly on insects they take larger prey as well. Some live above ground, others in burrows, and some spend part of the time in the water.

They are found on all the large land masses except Australia, Greenland, the southern half of South America and the polar regions.

Shrews

Shrews are secretive, mouselike animals with long, pointed snouts, short legs and tiny eyes often hidden beneath short, velvety fur. This hair is an adaptation to underground living because the hair is not rumpled no matter what direction the shrew moves in. Shrews are active year round and while most hunt after dark, there are some that hunt during the day as well. They are extremely nervous and high strung and can die from the shock of a sudden fright. Because their systems burn up food so fast they must eat almost continuously or starve to death.

The shrew family contains the smallest mammal in the world, the musk or dwarf shrew which weighs .08 ounce.

Shrews are cosmopolitan, living everywhere but the polar regions, Australia, Greenland and southern South America. There are seven species in New England.

Masked Shrew

Sorex cinereus cinereus

Restless, pugnacious and voracious are all good words to describe the masked shrew. With little provocation it will attack and eat its own kind.

Description: The masked shrew has a sharply pointed snout, beady eyes, small ears nearly hidden in fine, soft, thick, velvety fur. Its feet are delicate, each with five sharp, slender, weak claws. The tail is almost three-fourths the length of the head and body and covered with hair. The masked shrew is distinguished

MASKED SHREW

from the smoky shrew by its smaller size and lighter color, and from the least shrew by its much longer tail.

Its skull is narrow and fragile. Its front teeth are sharp and point forward. The tips of the teeth are dark chestnut color.

The hairs of the masked shrew are slate colored at the base. In winter the fur is dark brown to almost black on upper parts of the animal and lighter brown or grayish underneath. In summer the animal is lighter and browner. The feet are whitish. The tail is colored like the back on top and is yellowish below. Young masked shrews look much like their parents. Variants are rare, but albino and masked shrews with white patches have been reported. A spring molt takes place from April to June, and an autumn molt is usually completed in October.

Male and female masked shrews are the same size, 3.3 to 4.3 inches long, with a tail 1.8 to 1.4 inches. They weigh .12 to .21 of an ounce.

Distribution: The masked shrew is the most widely distributed shrew in North America. It occurs from Alaska through all of Canada, south in the Appalachian Mountains to North Carolina and Tennessee, in the northern half of the lower peninsula of Michigan, and through the mountains of Idaho, western Montana, and western Wyoming to northern New Mexico and to northeastern and central Washington.

Ecology: Living mainly in the woods beneath dead leaves, logs and rock piles, it prefers the cover of damp swamp bogs of spruce and cedar, hemlock ravines, mossy banks and mossy areas near streams that do not freeze or become stagnant. It is occasionally found in salt marshes but rarely in dry fields or woods. At times it lives in deserted buildings. It spends most of its time in underground runways and tunnels which were dug by mice and other small animals. Its nest, located in a hole under a log, stump, rock, or similar object, is a flattened sphere about 3 inches around made of leaves, grasses and tiny roots.

Larger mammal predators kill a lot of shrews but seldom eat them unless extremely hungry. Owls, hawks, herons, shrikes, weasels, foxes, cats and short-tailed shrews are known to kill masked shrews. Many die in floods, accidents or from being trapped in potholes, ditches, and springs. Extreme heat or cold and shock due to fright will also kill them. They are sometimes infested by ticks, fleas, chiggers and mites.

Behavior: Masked shrews are active day and night, but most active at dusk. They do not have sharp sight or smell, but their sense of touch is excellent. When discovered on the surface, they usually dive into a nearby tunnel, but when caught away from their holes (one researcher reports) they will quickly dig their way into loose sod, soon to reappear, giving a high-pitched call.

Masked shrews are good swimmers but don't often go into the water. While they are land animals they will climb low bushes, small branches and fallen trees. They travel about the surface of the ground by darting from tree to tree, poking their noses into crannies in constant search of food to keep up with their high energy demands. One masked shrew kept in captivity ate 3.3 times its own weight every 24 hours!

They are not known to store food. They eat a wide variety of insects, worms, centipedes, slugs, snails, mollusks, and spiders as well as vegetable matter such as moss and seeds, and the flesh of mice and other shrews.

Not much is known about their breeding habits. The breeding season may extend from March to September and the female may give birth to three litters a year. The young are probably born 18 days after conception and 2 to 10 are found in litters, the usual number being 7. At birth masked shrews are blind, naked and helpless. They grow rapidly, getting to half their adult size in about 10 days when they are fully furred with short hair. At a month old they are on their own. The male stays with the mother during the early life of the young. Sexual maturity is reached between 20 and 26 weeks, and masked shrews born in the spring probably produce their own young in the fall.

Water Shrew
Sorex palustris albibarbus

Description: This is the largest long-tailed shrew found in New England and it is specially adapted for aquatic life, with large hind feet with a short, stiff fringe of hairs and two of the toes joined by webbing for better swimming. The water shrew has beady eyes and small ears hidden in velvety fur. The nose is long, pointed and curves slightly down.

Both sexes of water shrew have similar color. In winter the

WATER SHREW

back is brown-black or gray-black with some hairs white-tipped. The underparts are grayish white. The tail is brownish black above and paler below. The outsides of the feet are dark and the insides whitish. In summer the water shrew is more brown on the back and lighter on the underside. It molts twice a year, during May or June and again in late August or September.

Males and females are the same size, ranging from 5.3 to 6.1 inches long with a tail 2.4 to 3.5 inches long. They weigh from .35 to .60 ounce.

Distribution: Water shrews are found from Nova Scotia and southern Quebec to British Columbia, the New England states, eastern and southwestern New York and south to northeastern Pennsylvania.

Ecology: Water shrews live along streams, ponds and lakes. They prefer heavily wooded areas and are rarely found in marshes. In winter they sometimes move into beaver lodges and muskrat houses. Dry moss is usually used for nest-making.

Weasels, mink, otters, hawks, owls, snakes, black bass, trout, pickerel and other fish eat water shrews.

Behavior: This is a secretive animal which seeks cover along the waterways it inhabits. Water shrews keep active during most of the winter and, while they are mostly night hunters, they sometimes move about at dusk, on dull, cloudy days and in shaded areas on sunny days. Their sense of sight seems poor, but smell and touch are highly developed. They swim easily and can dive, turn, twist, and run along the bottom, using all four feet in the same manner as when they run on the ground.

The water shrew may be small and fast enough to run across the surface of the water without breaking through. At least one researcher reported seeing one run more than 5 feet across the quiet surface of a pool, its entire body out of the water.

Water insects are their primary food source, mostly mayflies, caddis flies, stone flies, and water beetles. Snails, flatworms, small fish and fish eggs are also eaten.

Little is know about water shrew reproduction, but it appears that the breeding season lasts through most of the warm months. Birth is given after three weeks of gestation, with a litter usually having 4 to 8 young. They are thought to live about 18 months.

Smoky Shrew
Sorex fumeus

The smoky shrew apparently does not share the ravenous appetite which drives many of its relatives to frantic activity. Smoky shrews kept in captivity have not even managed to eat their own body weight daily. Insects are the staple of the smoky shrew's diet, but these animals also eat spiders, salamanders, snails, mammals, and birds.

Description: The smoky shrew looks like the masked shrew, but is bigger, heavier and darker. Its ears are bigger, its tail shorter, its feet bigger and somewhat lighter. The tail is brownish black above and yellow below. Old smoky shrews sometimes have white patches on the thighs or some white-tipped hairs.

SMOKY SHREW

The head is broad and short and the nose long and pointed. Smoky shrews get a coat of summer fur from April through June and convert to a winter coat between mid-September and early November.

Males and females are the same size, 3.7 to 5 inches long with a tail 1.4 to 2 inches.

Distribution: Smoky shrews are found from southern Ontario, through the east and north sides of the Saint Lawrence River, south from southern Maine, to most of New Hampshire, and Vermont, much of Massachusetts, Connecticut, and Rhode Island, west to central Ohio and Kentucky, and south to north-western Georgia.

Ecology: Basically a resident of the north and mountains, smoky shrews prefer cool, damp woods and bogs with deep, loose leaf cover. They nest up to a foot and a half underground beneath a stump or rotten log. The nest is the size of a baseball, lined with shredded grass, leaves and hair.

Short-tailed shrews, weasels, foxes, bobcats, owls, and hawks prey on smoky shrews.

Behavior: Not a great deal is known about the behavior of the smoky shrew. These animals are generally active all year at any hour. Their feet are too weak for effective digging and they use the runways of other small animals. They appear to have a breeding season from late March into early August. Birth occurs about 20 days after breeding with from 2 to 8 per litter, as many as three litters per season. Smoky shrews are born blind and naked and die of old age at 14 to 17 months.

Long-tailed Shrew
Sorex dispar dispar

Cold, deep evergreen forests and mountainous areas as high as 6,000 feet are the favored habitats of the long-tailed shrew.

Description: In appearance, the long-tailed shrew looks like the smoky shrew, only smaller, with a longer tail and a slate-gray

LONG-TAILED SHREW

coat worn year-round. The tail is brown-black above and paler below. They range from 3.9 to 5.3 inches long with a tail 2 to 2.3 inches long. Weight is .14 to .21 ounce.

Distribution: The long-tailed shrew is found in the mountains of Maine, south through western Massachusetts to eastern New York, central Pennsylvania and western New Jersey, and further south into North Carolina and Tennessee.

Ecology: The long-tailed shrew lives in depressions of moss-covered logs, in crevices of large mossy rock piles, among shaded, wooded rock slides, just beneath low, shaded cliffs, and at the edges of moist, grassy clearings surrounded by swampy woods. Its predators appear to be the same as those which hunt other shrews.

Behavior: Not much is known about the behavior of the long-tailed shrew, but biologists speculate that it is much the same as of other shrews living in similar habitats. Insects make up the bulk of its diet, along with spiders, centipedes and some plant material. Biologists know even less about the sex life of this shrew, although pregnant females have been found in May and August.

Thompson's Pygmy Shrew

Microsorex thompsoni thompsoni

This shrew has the distinction of being the smallest mammal found in New England, and it is among the smallest mammals in the world. It is from 3.2 to 3.8 inches long with a tail 1.1 to 1.3 inches, and weighs .08 to .13 ounce.

Description: Thompson's pygmy shrew is closely related to the long-tailed shrew, but has a shorter tail. It is easily confused with the masked shrew, but its skull is flatter and narrower.

Males and females are the same color. In summer they are reddish-brown or grayish brown above and smoky gray below. In winter they are olive-brown above and smoky gray below, occasionally tinged with light buff. The tail is two-colored, brown above and paler below, darker toward the tip.

Distribution: Thompson's pygmy shrew is found from the Gaspe Penninsula to southern Wisconsin, south of the Great Lakes, and extends southward along the Allegheny-Appalachian Mountains into northern Georgia.

Ecology: These shrews are often found in wet, or mingled wet and dry, habitats. They spend much time under old stumps and rotting logs, and among the litter of sedges, ferns, clumps of aspens, beech-maple forests, and in heavy spruce and pine bordering water. Their enemies are the same as other shrews.

Behavior: One captive Thompson's pygmy shrew would sit on its hind legs like a kangaroo and emit whistling sounds. It gave off a powerful musk when excited and moved so fast that at times it became a blur. Generally most active at night, this shrew moves around in the day as well. Nothing is known of its reproductive habits.

Short-tailed Shrew
Blarina brevicauda

As far as is known, the short-tailed shrew is the only mammal with a poisonous bite. It secretes a venom from glands located between the lower incisor teeth. Mixed with saliva, this venom seeps into the wound from a groove between the long teeth, paralyzing its prey.

A small amount of this venom is potent enough to kill a rabbit. One scientist, bitten on the fingers while holding a short-tailed shrew, suffered shooting pains and swelling which in half an hour reached his elbow. The pain was so great he could not use one of his hands for three days.

The venom of the short-tailed shrew seems to work in much

SHORT-TAILED SHREW

the same fashion as the poison of a cobra.

Description: The short-tailed shrew is larger and more robust than its other New England relatives. It can be recognized by its short, scantily-haired tail, less than half the length of the head and body. Its eyes are beady and its small ears are hidden in fur. The legs are short and the five-clawed feet are broad and large. A pair of scent glands on the flanks are more developed in males.

Males and females have the same color, in winter dark slate above and paler below and in summer slightly lighter. The tail is darker on top. Albinos and all-white short-tailed shrews occur rarely. These shrews change coats twice a year, in May or June and again in November. They range from 4.1 to 5.2 inches long with a tail from .7 to 1.2 inches. Weight is from .44 to .82 ounce.

Distribution: The short-tailed variety is one of the commonest shrews in the eastern United States and southeastern Canada. It ranges from Nova Scotia west into Manitoba, and south through eastern Colorado and southeastern Texas into Florida.

Ecology: One of the most abundant animals in New England, the short-tailed shrew lives in nearly all habitats. It is found in woods where it tunnels under leaves, moss, and loose loam in search of food. It also is found along the banks of small streams, under logs, brush piles and in tall, rank grass. It will live in the tunnels of other small mammals or in log cavities, old stumps, building crevices and stone walls.

Short-tailed shrews build resting nests, 6 to 7 inches long, on runways or under stumps, rocks or logs, and more elaborate mating nests, 6 to 10 inches long. The nests are made of shredded grass and leaves and usually have 3 openings, one at the bottom for escape and one on either end for burrow access.

They have many enemies, but few mammals eat them, probably because of their musky odor. Fleas, mites and other parasites infest them. Many shrews die from floods, starvation, temperature changes, accidents, and fights with other shrews.

Behavior: Short-tailed shrews are active any time of day or night, all year long, but like cloudy, damp days best. They are extremely nervous, aggressive, and endlessly active. In the wild they are belligerent towards other shrews.

They crawl beneath leaf mold during day and come above

ground at night. In winter they burrow through snow. They can only run about three miles an hour, but they run constantly, and sometimes leap. When pressed, they'll swim.

It takes a lot of energy for that sort of behavior. Their heartbeat has been recorded at 760 beats per minutes and average breathing at 164 breaths a minute.

Voracious eaters, they feed mainly on insects, the young of insects, and earthworms, but they also take larger game such as salamanders, snakes, songbirds, mice, voles, young hares and rabbits, and other shrews. They will also eat berries, fruits, nuts, and roots. They cache food in small storage areas in their tunnels.

The short-tailed shrew follows through with its super-active lifestyle when it comes to reproduction, mating as many as 20 times a day during a mating season in late winter. The young are born 21 or 22 days after the mating, with between 3 and 10 per litter. At birth they are blind and helpless, measure about an inch long, and weigh a gram. The young shrews leave the nest between 18 and 20 days old and are weaned by the 25th day. They live for 18 to 20 months.

Short-tailed shrews have poor eyesight and moderate ability to smell, but fine senses of hearing and touch. When happy or feeding they make a musical twitter like a sparrow. When scared or angry they make a shrill grating note or high-pitched chatter.

Least Shrew
Cryptotis parva

For its kind, the least shrew is a remarkably social animal. Groups of up to 30 will gather to build tunnels and nests which they share during the nesting and winter seasons. But when food is scarce, they revert to the aggressive nature of other shrews and may resort to cannibalism.

Description: The least shrew looks like a smaller version of the short-tailed shrew, with a long, pointed snout. It has beady black eyes and tiny ears almost hidden in velvety fur. The tail is slender and less than half the length of the body and head. Each foot has 5 toes. It has 30 teeth, rather than the 32 of other shrews.

Male and female least shrews are alike in color. The back is dark brown and the underparts ash gray; the color is somewhat paler in summer. Least shrews molt twice a year, in April or May and again in September or October.

The least shrew is from 2.7 to 3.5 inches long with a tail .47 to .78 inch. Weights vary from .14 to .20 ounce.

Distribution: They are found from western coastal Connecticut to central New York, west to South Dakota, south to west and central Texas and the Gulf of Mexico, and east into Florida.

Ecology: Least shrews favor dry, grassy fields, such as old pastures along edges of woods. They use the burrows of moles, voles and other small mammals, but will make their own in soft soil. They build a nest in a shallow depression of a burrow, under a stump, rock, small boxes or cans, or other objects. The nest is roughly round, 2 to 5 inches in diameter, and made of shredded grass or other fine material.

Owls, hawks, foxes, cats, short-tailed shrews and snakes are known to kill least shrews.

Behavior: They are restless, nervous and active throughout the year, at all hours, but mainly at night. They move with arched back in quick, jerky motions.

The least shrew hunts mostly by touch and to a lesser extent with smell. These animals do not have good hearing or vision. When alarmed they give sharp, high squeals. They spend a lot of time washing and combing their fur. They can swim, but they avoid water.

Least shrews are big eaters and dine on insects, earthworms, centipedes, millipedes, snails, salamanders, the remains of mice and other small mammals, and some plant material. They like to eat frogs which they catch by hamstringing the hind legs. They are reported to raid beehives where they eat the bees and sometimes build a nest.

Breeding season for the least shrew is from mid-March to November. Birth occurs in 15 days or less after mating. Litters range from 3 to 6. Females have been known to give birth, raise and wean a litter, then give birth to another litter, all within 24 days. The young are born blind and naked and less than an inch long. They grow rapidly, and by the 9th day they are fully furred. They are weaned by the time they are 21 days old. One captive least shrew lived to be 21 months old.

Moles

The moles are a family of animals highly adapted for underground living, although some kinds are amphibious or semiaquatic.

Moles have oversized, powerful shoulders and front legs. The handlike front feet are designed for digging in soil. Moles have round bodies, narrow in the hips to enable the mole to turn in a tunnel. They have long, probing snouts and tiny ears hidden in short, velvety fur.

Moles are active year round and basically eat insects, although some species also eat plants. Members of the family are found in the temperate parts of North America and Eurasia.

Hairy-tailed Mole

Parascalops breweri

The hairy-tailed mole would have to be included among any lists
of champion eaters. A captive male weighing 1.8 ounces ate 2.3
ounces of earthworms and larvae in just 24 hours.

Description: As the name implies, this mole has a furry tail,
unlike the eastern mole with a naked tail. The large forefeet are
almost round in outline and the toes are not webbed. Females
have eight nipples.

Males and females are alike in color, dark slate to black above
and a little paler below. Some have a small white spot on the
breast or abdomen.

Males average larger than females. Adults are 5.5 to 6 inches
long and weigh 1.4 to 2.2 ounces.

Distribution: Hairy-tailed moles are found from New Brunswick, southeastern Canada, into eastern Ontario, south through
eastern Ohio, and in the Appalachian mountains to western
North Carolina.

Ecology: They live in woods and meadows with loose, well-
drained soil. They are found both at high elevations and near sea
level.

The tunnels made by hairy-tailed moles are irregular and complex, less visible from the surface than those made by the eastern

HAIRY-TAILED MOLE

mole. Winter tunnels are from 10 to 20 inches below surface. The nest is about 6 inches around and lined with dry grass and leaves.

Foxes, cats, weasels, owls, hawks and snakes prey on hairy-tailed moles. They suffer from fleas, lice and internal parasites.

Behavior: Hairy-tailed moles are active at all hours and come above ground at night. They have been observed swimming.

They are voracious eaters, consuming earthworms, insects and their young, millipedes, centipedes, snails and slugs.

Breeding is in March and April and four or five young are born about a month later, blind and naked. They are weaned and on their own in another month.

Eastern Mole

Scalopus aquaticus aquaticus

The concern of homeowners who find their lawns invaded by eastern moles is well taken. Their just-under-the-surface burrows are dug at a rate of 10 to 20 feet an hour, and during wet weather their digging may average 100 to 150 feet a day.

Description: The eastern mole has a stout, round body with a pointed snout on one end and a short, naked tail on the other. It has tiny eyes covered by thin skin. Both eyes and ears are hidden in fur. Its front feet are lightly haired and out-sized, wider than they are long, with heavy claws for digging. Normally the front feet are held outward with the palms vertical. In sharp contrast, the hind feet are small and weak with one to three tubercles on each. Front and hind feet are webbed. The tail is short, thick and round. The fur is soft, dense and velvety. Females have six nipples.

Both males and females have the same colors, black to brownish above and paler below. They are lighter in summer than in winter. Young are much grayer than adults. Some eastern moles have been found colored all-white, orange, and cream, with some having yellow blotches on the belly. They molt in late summer or early fall and again in early spring. Males are slightly bigger than females. Adults are from 5.7 to 8 inches long and weigh 1.8 to 4.2 ounces.

Distribution: Eastern moles live in the eastern United States from Massachusetts west to eastern Wyoming and Colorado, south to central Texas and the Gulf of Mexico.

Ecology: Open woodlands, meadows, pastures, cultivated fields, gardens and lawns that are well-drained with sandy or light loam soils are home for the eastern mole. Soil which has earthworms and will support tunnel-building is the requirement.

They dig tunnels with alternate thrusts of their forepaws, pushing dirt behind the body where it is kicked further behind. The eastern mole rotates its body about 45 degrees to each side while digging, forcing the soil upward, creating the ridges that often mar lawns.

Its nest is located a foot or more underground and is a chamber about 5 inches wide and 8 inches long lined with tiny roots or grass and sometimes leaves.

Man, weasels, short-tailed shrews, foxes, dogs, cats, skunks, owls, and snakes prey on eastern moles. They have fleas, lice and a variety of internal parasites.

Behavior: Eastern moles are solitary except during breeding season, which is from March through April. The young are born 42 to 45 days after mating with litters of 2 to 5. The newborn are pink, blind and helpless, but leave the nest on their own at 4 weeks.

They are active all year long, day and night. They spend most of their lives underground, but they do come out at night. They don't like water but are good swimmers. They are quiet, but squeal shrilly when disturbed.

Their food is chiefly earthworms, beetles, grubs, centipedes, millipedes, wireworms, ants, spiders, slugs and insects. They also eat vegetable matter at times.

Star-nosed Mole
Condylura cristata

Identification is simple and positive with the star-nosed mole: No other mammal has 22 pink tentacles arranged in a starry circle around its snout. These sensitive feelers form a wide nasal disk, with 11 points on either side of a vertical line dividing the snout.

Description: In winter the star-nosed mole's tail is swollen and covered with coarse black hairs. It is possible that the tail fat serves as food for the breeding season. The females have eight nipples.

Males and females are blackish brown or nearly black above and browner and paler below. The tail is lighter on the underside. Young are paler than adults. They molt in June and July and again in September and October.

Adults are from 6.8 to 8.1 inches long with a tail 2.7 to 3.3 inches long. They weigh 1.4 to 2.7 ounces.

STAR-NOSED MOLE

Distribution: Star-nosed moles are found from southern Labrador across southeastern Canada to southwestern Manitoba, south through the lake state to Illinois, Indiana, and Ohio, and from the northeastern United States south in the Appalachian Mountains to western North Carolina.

Ecology: They prefer deep, mucky soil in low, wet meadows, bogs, marshes and swamps. Sometimes they are found near streams and ponds and in damp spots in fields.

Star-nosed moles make irregular burrows which may branch around rocks and trees, and which may go two feet deep in one area, rise to the surface at another, and end at or below the water level of a stream. Mice, shrews and other small mammals share these burrows. The ridges made by star-nosed moles are about 1 ¾ inches wide by 1 ½ inches high. The nest is a flattened sphere 5 to 7 inches in diameter and 3 to 5 inches high, built well above high-water level beneath a stump, log or fallen tree and lined with grass, straw and leaves.

Hawks, owls, dogs, foxes, weasels, mink, snakes, pickerel, pike, muskelunge, and black bass eat them. They have fleas and mites and various internal parasites.

Behavior: Active day and night, year-round, star-nosed moles burrow in snow and even travel on its surface. They burrow at a rate 7 to 8 feet an hour and can run 4 or 5 miles per hour.

Star-nosed moles are good swimmers and use their front feet like oars while sculling with their tails. They also dive underwater.

They eat aquatic insects, earthworms, crustaceans, slugs, snails, an occasional small minnow, and some plant material.

They live in small colonies, and seem to pair off in the fall and remain together until the young are born. Birth takes place about 45 days after mating, with 3 to 7 young born naked, blind, and helpless in May or June. The newborn are about 2 inches long and are weaned and on their own at 3 weeks. By August or September they reach adult size.

3. Mammals That Fly

*T*HE BATS, known to biologists as the order Chiroptera, are the only mammals that fly. The finger bones are thin and long and covered by an elastic, leathery membrane which grows from the sides of the body, legs and tail, forming wings. The thumbs are free of the wings, have claws, and are used for grasping. Bat knees are directed outward and back; this allows the bat to hang upside down by its toes. Bats can launch themselves into flight by releasing their toeholds and spreading their wings.

Bats have small eyes, but large, well-developed ears. In flight bats are guided by echoes received from their supersonic cries. They use these echoes to avoid obstacles and to find flying prey.

Most bats are highly social, but as a rule the sexes separate in summer. They are active at dawn and dusk, or at night, and sleep the day away in dark places, in the foliage of trees or in caves. Some kinds migrate south in the fall where most hibernate in caves. Some bats eat insects, others eat nectar, fruit, fish, meat, and even blood.

Bats live in all the temperate and tropical areas of the world, except for a few small, remote islands.

Common Bats

The common bats, the only type found in New England, are small to middle-sized. Their faces lack the leaflike growths of some species and their tails reach to the back edge of the tail membrane, but not much beyond. They have small teeth.

These bats are mainly insect eaters, capturing food in flight, on the ground, and over water. They may roost singly, in pairs, in small groups, or in large colonies during the entire year, but some gather only in winter. Some types of bats migrate between summer and winter roosts, usually returning to the same locations each season.

Little Brown Myotis

Myotis lucifugus

The little brown myotis might be described as a winged insect-catching machine. It has been observed catching flies on the wing at the rate of one every 3 ½ seconds!

Description: The little brown myotis has a hairy face, beady black eyes, a broad, blunt nose, and short, rounded, naked ears. The wing membrane is attached to the foot near the base of the toes. Long hairs extend beyond the sharp claws. The tip of the tail is usually free of the wing membrane. Females have 2 nipples.

The fur is dense, fine and glossy. Males and females are alike in color, rich brown with a dark spot on the shoulders. The ears and wing membranes are dark brown and glossy. The young are darker and grayer. White-blotched and almost completely black little brown myotis have been reported.

Females are slightly larger than males. Adults are 3.1 to 3.7 inches long with a tail 1.4 to 1.7 inches. Wingspread ranges from 8.6 to 10.5 inches. They weigh from .25 to .35 ounce.

Distribution: They are found from Labrador to southern Alaska, south in the southern mountains of California, and in the Appalachians to Georgia and west into Arkansas. This is one of the most abundant bats in the northern parts of its range.

Ecology: Little brown myotis are found almost everywhere. In spring and summer, females form colonies of hundreds in attics, barns, and other dark, hot places. Solitary males roost in cooler, more exposed places, such as under tree bark.

In late summer, the female colonies break up and both sexes roost in trees and dark places. In winter they hibernate in caves and mines. They return to the same roosting and hibernating locations each season.

Hibernation ends in early April to mid-May for females and early May to early June for males. They return to their hibernation caves in September and October.

Man, cats, mink, raccoons, hawks, owls, red-winged blackbirds, common grackles, rat snakes, leopard frogs and black bass have been known to catch little brown myotis. They suffer from fleas, wing mites and a large blood-sucking bat bug, *Cimex pilosellus*. They have internal parasites, and some become infested with rabies.

Behavior: Shortly after dusk, little brown myotis fly to water where they skim the surface to drink and catch insects. They also feed over lawns and fields, or among trees near their roost. These bats land with head up, bank slightly, then hook the claws of the

Mammals That Fly

thumbs and hind feet to catch hold and quickly turn head down to hang by the hind feet.

They fly at 12.5 to 21.7 miles an hour, and in experiments blindfolded bats got home as quickly as sighted bats from a distance of 5 miles. Banded bats have found their way home when released 70 miles away.

Little brown myotis are awkward on ground, but swim fairly well. They issue a wide variety of sounds from squeaks to supersonic cries.

As a bat takes wing, it emits cries at about 30 kilocycles per second. When it nears an object, this increases to 50 kilocycles. The bat judges its distance from the object by sensing the time delay between the outgoing sound and the return of the echo. The bat is prevented from hearing its own cry by a minute ear muscle that closes as the cry is emitted. For an object 6 inches from the bat's mouth, the time delay for an echo is about a thousandth of a second, and a bat can detect a mosquito that quickly from the echo.

They are voracious eaters, taking all kinds of winged insects. They regularly catch insects with their wings or tail and transfer them to the mouth, all within a half second. From the time a bat eats an insect to the time it eliminates the remains is as little as 35 minutes, and it will often have a full stomach an hour after starting to hunt.

Little brown myotis usually mate in the fall prior to hibernation. The female stores the sperm in her uterus during the winter and the eggs are fertilized when she emerges from hibernation. The babies are born 50 to 60 days later, usually one to a mother. The mother carries her young for the first three or four days as she hunts. The young are weaned in two or three weeks and can fly at 3 to 4 weeks. Colonies disband as soon as the young can feed themselves.

Keen's Myotis
Myotis keenii septentrionalis

Description: Keen's myotis looks like a little brown myotis in size and color, but has a longer tail and narrower and longer ears which extend beyond the tip of the nose when laid forward. They arc brown but not glossy, and the young are grayer than adults. Females have 2 nipples.

Males and females are similar in size, 3 to 3.7 inches long with a tail 1.4 to 1.6 inches and wingspread of 9 to 10.7 inches. They weigh .25 to .32 ounce.

Distribution: This bat is found in eastern North America, from Newfoundland, Nova Scotia, across southern Canada to west central Saskatchewan, South to northern Florida, and west to Wyoming.

Ecology and Behavior: Little is known about these bats. They roost singly or in small colonies in caves, under loose bark, behind window shutters, in cliff crevices and around cave mouths in summer. They form nursery colonies in attics, barn roofs and tree cavities. They have been found hibernating in mines and caves.

Feeding habits are probably the same as those of the little brown myotis. Little is known about its reproduction. Its life span may be at least 18 years.

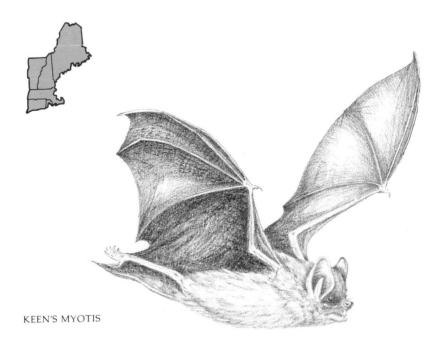

KEEN'S MYOTIS

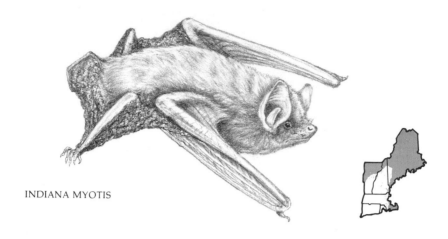

INDIANA MYOTIS

Indiana Myotis
Myotis sodalis

Homing instinct is exceptionally strong in Indiana myotis. These bats have been able to find their way home when researchers have taken them 200 miles from their caves.

Description: The Indiana myotis looks like the little brown myotis, with a slightly longer tail and smaller, more delicate hind feet. It differs in color having gray-chestnut fur. Adults molt once a year during mid-June. Variants are rare but white-spotted individuals have been seen.

Males and females are the same size, 2.9 to 3.7 inches long with a tail 1.8 to 1.2 inches long and a wingspread of 9.4 to 10.3 inches. They weigh from .18 to .28 ounce.

Distribution: They are found in the eastern United States from central New England west to Wisconsin, Missouri, and Arkansas, and south into northern Florida.

Ecology: The Indiana myotis may be no longer present in New England and will probably disappear in the future unless its hibernation caves are given protection. It is on the U.S. Department of the Interior's endangered species list.

These bats disperse widely in the summer, living in caves, but in winter they congregate in just a few caves. It is estimated that

97% of the Indiana myotis hibernate in certain large caves in Kentucky, Missouri, Indiana and Illinois.

Adult females summer singly or in small groups and bear their young in hollow trees or under loose bark.

Man, cats, hawks, owls and snakes prey on Indiana myotis. Cave floodings may kill thousands of them.

Behavior: Indiana myotis begin to enter hibernation caves about mid-September. During hibernation they wake every 8 to 10 days and form squeaking clusters in deeper parts of the cave where it is warmer. They stay awake for about an hour at these times. In cold weather they form tight clusters, with the wings folded tightly about their bodies. In spring most females leave the cave first.

The feeding habits of this bat are believed to be similar to those of the little brown myotis. Known facts about its reproduction are scarce, but it appears to produce a single offspring in late June. They live to 12 years or more.

Small-footed Myotis
Myotis leibii leibii

Caves in the foothills of mountains to 2,000 feet with hemlock, spruce and white cedar seem to be the habitat of the small-footed myotis.

Description: This bat looks like the little brown mytois but has golden-tinted, almost yellow fur and shorter forearms. It is recognized by a black facial mask, black ears, and a lack of dark shoulder patches. Its skull is much flatter than that of the little brown myotis.

Male and female are equal size, 2.8 to 3.3 inches long with a tail 1.2 to 1.5 inches long and with a wingspread of 8.3 to 9.7 inches. They weigh .18 to .28 ounce.

Distribution: They are found from Ontario and southwestern Quebec south into the mountains of northern Georgia and west to Arkansas, Missouri and southern Iowa and eastern Kansas. It is one of the least common bats in the eastern part of its range.

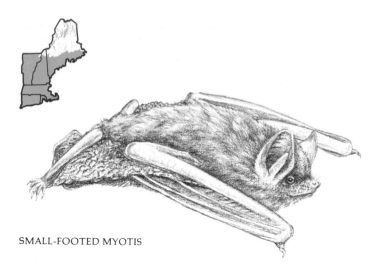

SMALL-FOOTED MYOTIS

Ecology: The small-footed myotis roosts in buildings and beneath rock slabs in summer. In winter it lives in mines and caves.

Behavior: A hardy bat, the small-footed myotis enters hibernating caves before mid-November and leaves by March. They hibernate in narrow cracks, singly and in groups up to 50 or more. Little is known about their feeding or breeding habits. Maternity colonies of 12 to 20 have been found in buildings, and they seem to have a single offspring per year. They are known to live to at least 12 years old.

Silver-haired Bat
Lasionycteris moctivagans

Silver-haired bats are strong flyers that don't hesitate to cross open water on migration flights. A male was found on a research ship 95 miles south-southeast of Montauk Point, Long Island. A banded male flew 107 miles in 14 days.

Description: A medium-sized bat, the silver-haired has short, naked, rounded ears nearly as broad as long. The wing membrane is attached to the base of the toes. The fur is long and soft. Males and females are alike in color, blackish brown on the sides and back; the hairs are strongly tipped with silver-white, and this gives these bats a bright silvery appearance. The belly is slightly lighter than the back, and the head, neck and throat are black. Both sexes are the same size, 3.7 to 4.5 inches long with a tail 1.4 to 2 inches long, and have a wingspread of 10.5 to 12.1 inches. They weigh .25 to .35 ounce.

Distribution: The silver-haired bat occurs throughout North America from Alaska across southern Canada, and south through all the states except perhaps Florida.

Ecology: These bats live in woodlands bordering lakes and streams. Population is erratic, numerous in some areas and scarce in others. Silver-haired bats roost in dense tree foliage and in tree hollows, old crows' nests, or woodpecker holes, or under loose bark. During migrations they can be found in buildings, quarries, fenceposts, slab and lumber piles, or ship hulls. Occasionally they enter caves and mines.

Man, owls, hawks, and striped skunks are their enemies.

Behavior: Silver-haired bats fly earlier than most bats, even before sunset. They are slow, erratic flyers, gliding frequently while darting among trees, over woodland streams and ponds at

SILVER-HAIRED BAT

heights of 20 feet.

They are sociable and sometimes form large groups. One colony of 300 was reported behind a closed window shutter, and a colony of 10,000 was discovered living in a Maryland house.

They are believed to feed entirely on nocturnal insects, especially those that fly high over the borders of woodland streams and ponds.

One litter, usually of two young, is born in early June or late July. The newborn are black, wrinkled and nearly hairless. They grow rapidly and cling to the mother until about 3 weeks old when they are able to fly.

Eastern Pipistrelle
Pipistrellus subflavus obscurus

The eastern pipistrelle inhabits more caves in the eastern United States than any other species.

Description: One of the smallest bats in New England, it is the only one with 34 teeth. It has yellowish brown, tricolor fur which is lead gray at the base, then yellowish brown and tipped with dark brown. The wing membranes are blackish, the ears tan. The body appears dark brown above, yellowish brown below. Nearly

EASTERN PIPISTRELLE

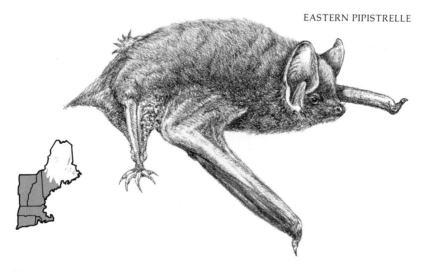

all-white and black eastern pipistrelles occur rarely.

Males and females are the same size, 2.9 to 3.5 inches long with a tail 1.4 to 1.8 inches long, and a wingspread of 8.1 to 10.1 inches. They weigh .14 to .25 ounce.

Distribution: They are found in eastern North America from southern Quebec and Nova Scotia, west to Minnesota, south to Oklahoma and to eastern Mexico, Guatemala, and Honduras.

Ecology: This wide-ranging bat is usually found in small clusters in open woods near water, in cliff crevices and rocks, and sometimes in caves and buildings in the summer. In spring and summer it is sometimes found hanging singly in abandoned buildings, porch roofs and lofts. It hibernates in caves, mines and rock crevices.

Behavior: A dainty little bat, it is a weak flyer and can be mistaken for a large, fluttering moth. It begins to fly in early evening at treetop level, often covering such a small area that it stays constantly in sight. It often feeds over ponds and streams. It has been clocked as flying at 11.7 miles an hour and has found its home from 85 miles away.

Fat pipistrelles enter hibernating caves in mid-October and remain until late April, females departing before males. They hibernate deeply, sleeping in one position for a week or more to awaken, fly about for a while, and return to the same spots.

Pipistrelles feed on flies, grain moths, and smaller bugs and beetles. They are able to fill their stomachs within 20 minutes of starting to hunt.

Breeding is in November, and a litter of two young is produced in mid-June to mid-July. The young can fly at one month old. Females live about 10 years and males 15.

Big Brown Bat
Eptesicus fuscus

The big brown bat is the one most often seen by man because it commonly frequents his structures. In summer it roosts in attics, belfries, barns, behind shutters, awnings and doors, in hollow trees and beneath bridges. In winter it hibernates in buildings, caves, mines, storm sewers and other retreats.

Description: The second largest New England bat, the big brown bat has a uniformly dark brown fur. Each hair is blackish on its lower half, the outer half brown. The face, ears and wings are blackish. Males and females look alike. Albinos, white-splotched and pied big browns have been reported.

The ears are short, rounded and naked and barely reach the nose when laid forward. The large skull is heavy. Sizes range from 4.1 to 4.8 inches, with a tail 1.6 to 2 inches long and a wingspread of 12.1 to 12.9 inches. They weigh .42 to .56 ounce.

Distribution: Big brown bats are found from Alaska and southern Canada south to northern South America, including the Caribbean Islands. They have not been reported in southern Florida or much of central Texas.

Ecology: Big brown bats are hardy and can stand nearly freezing temperatures.

Man, great horned owls, barn owls, screech owls, sparrow hawks, common grackles, cats, and snakes kill them. They have mites, fleas, blood-sucking bugs and internal parasites. Rabies is reportedly more common in big brown bats than in little brown myotis.

Behavior: They do not form into large colonies as some bats do, with the average grouping well under 200. They take wing at dusk, but are sometimes seen flying at midday. They fly a nearly straight course at a height of 20 to 30 feet, and their average speed is reported at 10.4 miles per hour. Big brown bats are easy to identify in flight because of their large size, slow wing beats and audible chatter. When captured they are vicious and can inflict a painful bite. They are not known to migrate far from the place they are born.

Big brown bats have remarkable homing ability. Captured and released 250 miles away from home, all of a group of them found their way home by the fifth night. They have found their homes after being taken 450 miles away.

They hibernate late and are seen flying in November, and in early March. They hibernate in caves and mines, with the males in tight clusters and the females hanging singly.

BIG BROWN BAT

Most of their food is insects.

Breeding takes place in the fall and winter, and sperm are stored in the female until the first week of April when the eggs are fertilized. The usual two young are born two months later, naked and blind and weighing .14 ounce. The young are weaned in three weeks and able to fly by early July. They live more than 10 years.

Red Bat
Lasiurus borealis

Strong flyers, red bats have been clocked going nearly 40 miles an hour on straightaway flight.

Description: Bright, rusty coloration makes the red bat easy to identify. It has short, rounded ears and long, pointed wings. It

RED BAT

sticks its long tail straight out in flight. The females have four nipples. Males tend to be redder and less frosted on the back than females. The wings are brownish black. They are not known to molt.

Females are slightly larger. Adults are 3.7 to 4.8 inches long with a tail 1.6 to 2.1 inches long and a wingspread fo 11.3 to 12.9 inches. They weigh .28 to .49 ounce.

Distribution: Red bats are found widely over North America, from Nova Scotia and New Brunswick across southern Canada to Alberta and south to Texas and Florida, from British Columbia south to Panama, but not the Rocky Mountains and the central plateau of Mexico.

Ecology: Red bats roost in trees, usually on the south side and sometimes near the ground, hiding in the leaves. They are rarely found in caves or buildings.

It is said that blue jays feed heavily on young red bats, and they are the prey of hawks, owls, cats, opossums, skunks and tree-climbing snakes. Fleas, bat bugs and internal parasites inflict them. Rabies has been confirmed in red bats.

Behavior: Red bats fly at dusk; their flight is usually slow and erratic. Infrequently they will fly during the day. They hunt 600 to 1,000 yards from the roosting site. They frequently give sharp chirps when flying.

Red bats are known to eat flying moths, flies, bugs, beetles, crickets and cicadas.

Breeding is from August to October. Fertilization occurs in the spring after the bats emerge from hibernation, and the young are born in late May to early July. Red bats have large litters for bats—up to five young which are born blind, naked and helpless. They can fly at 3 to 4 weeks and are weaned at 5 to 6 weeks. They live to 12 years.

Hoary Bat
Lasiurus cinereus

The largest and most strikingly colored New England bat is the hoary bat with its dark brown fur tinged heavily with white, giving a frosty appearance.

Description: Hoary bat fur is brownish-black at the base, followed by a band of yellowish brown and white at the tip. The

HOARY BAT

49

cheeks and throat are yellowish, and the ears are tan rimmed with black or dark brown. The wings are brownish black. Males and females look alike, and they are not known to molt. The ears are large and rounded. Females have 4 nipples, and are larger than males.

They are from 5.1 to 5.9 inches long, with a tail 2 to 2.4 inches long and a wingspread of 14.6 to 16.4 inches. They weigh from .88 to 1.58 ounces.

Distribution: This is the most widespread North American bat, ranging from the tundra of Southampton Island southward in Canada from the Atlantic to the Pacific, south into South America into Chile, and to the Dominican Republic and Bermuda. It is rare in the eastern United States.

Ecology: Hoary bats roost in trees and prefer evergreens, 10 to 15 feet above ground. They sometimes wander into caves in summer.

Man and occasionally hawks and owls prey on hoary bats. They are known to carry rabies.

Behavior: Hoary bats usually take wing late in the evening, but on cooler evenings may fly before dark. They are strong flyers and may be able to reach 60 miles an hour. They usually migrate south in cold weather along with red and silver-haired bats. They make audible chattering sounds when migrating.

Insects are the primary food of hoary bats, but they also eat pipistrelles.

The young are born from mid-May into early July. The litter is usually two young, and they are born blind and naked, weighing .18 ounce. Within a month they are able to fly and care for themselves.

4. Hoppers and Leapers

*P*IKAS, HARES AND RABBITS all belong to a group of animals called Lagomorphs. At one time they were classed with rodents, but they differ in having an upper pair of small incisor teeth directly behind the large front ones. These teeth are nearly circular in outline and don't have cutting edges.

These ground animals run on their toes but hop flat on the entire foot. They are strict plant eaters. Some kinds re-eat their own fecal pellets, apparently to aid in bacterial digestion of the plant material, for much the same reason a cow chews its cud.

Man has transplanted rabbits and hares all over the world, with the exception of Antarctica and a few small, remote islands.

Rabbits and Hares

People commonly use the terms hare and rabbit as if they refer to the same animal. They don't. Newborn hares are well-furred, have their eyes open, and can run shortly after being born. Rabbits are born naked and helpless, with their eyes closed. Rabbits are born in a nest well-hidden in a depression; hares are born in simply a sheltered spot. Rabbits use burrows; hares don't. Hares are larger than rabbits and have outsized ears and legs. They are much stronger runners than rabbits.

Both rabbits and hares have excellent hearing and large eyes on the sides of their heads to detect danger from any angle. Their back legs are much longer and more powerful than the front. They have cleft upper lips. They are most active at twilight times.

Eastern Cottontail
Sylvilagus floridanus

The eastern cottontail is not a native New Englander but was probably first introduced to Nantucket Island before 1900.

Description: The eastern cottontail has dense fur on the soles of its feet, with five toes on the front foot and four on the hind foot. The tail is short, thick and fluffy.

Its fur is long and coarse. Males and females are the same color and change coats only slightly with the seasons. The upper parts vary from reddish brown mixed with black to grayish brown, except for a cinnamon-rust nape. The face and flanks are grayish and the chest brownish, while the underparts are white. The legs are a rich cinnamon-rufous color. The outside of the ear is buffy gray, bordered by a thin black strip at the front and tip. The hind feet are pale rusty buff to white above. The tail is brownish above, white below. There is a white ring around the eyes.

A white spot occurs on the forehead of 50% of eastern cottontails; others have a light brown spot. The eye is deep brown and reflects a brilliant red in bright light. Albino, all-white and black cottontails are rare.

Adult cottontails undergo a continuous molt from February to

EASTERN COTTONTAIL

November with two distinct phases: a spring molt from March to August and a fall molt from September to November.

The females are larger than males. Adults are 14.8 to 18 inches long with a tail 1.2 to 1.7 inches. The hind foot is 3 to 4.1 inches long. They weigh 1.8 to 2.95 pounds.

Distribution: Eastern cottontails are found throughout the eastern United States and extreme southern Canada and south through eastern Mexico, parts of Yucatan, and Central America, with a separated population in Texas, New Mexico and Arizona.

In New England they are found in western Vermont from the Massachusetts border to the Canadian border, in the southern portions of New Hampshire, throughout Connecticut and Rhode Island, and in Massachusetts except for a narrow belt in the central northern section.

Ecology: Eastern cottontails are found in fields, meadows, farmlands, dense high grass, wood thickets, along fencerows, overgrown stone walls, forest edges, and the edges of sedge swamps and marshes.

Most of the day is spent resting in "forms" concealed in dense

Hoppers and Leapers   53

grass, weed patches, hay fields, along roadsides, in scrubby woods and thickets. They make the form by scratching or tramping the ground. The forms range from 6 to 11 inches long. In stormy or cold weather cottontails hide in dens, brushpiles, stone walls, grain shocks, and burrows.

A pregnant female digs a nest into the ground and lines and covers it with grass and fur plucked from her body. Although cottontails do not dig burrows, they take advantage of abandoned woodchuck burrows, rock crevices and hollow logs. They prefer dry areas, but may stay in swamps and marshes in hot weather.

Man, dogs, foxes, coyotes, bobcats, cats, weasels, raccoons, mink, owls, hawks, crows and snakes prey on cottontails. Fires, floods, farm machinery and extreme cold kills many. They have fleas, lice, ticks and internal parasites. Rabbits are victims of tularemia or "rabbit sickness."

Behavior: Active mainly at night and early morning, they are about all year round except during heavy snow, during storms, or sudden temperature drops.

Cottontails are solitary, except for females with young. Wary, they flush easily from hiding places. They are timid but will kick and scratch with their strong hind feet if caught. They are usually silent, although females with young sometimes grunt. When caught or terrified they give a shrill cry. When playing, breeding or fighting, they make low purring, grunting or growling sounds. Most thump the ground with their hind feet. They can swim but avoid water. They normally move along in short hops and jumps. They can move at up to 18 miles an hour.

The home range of a cottontail is from a half acre to more than 40 acres, depending on habitat, season, age and sex of the rabbit.

They eat almost any kind of green vegetation, including bark, twigs, and buds of woody plants.

The breeding season may extend from mid-February through September. The young are born 30 days after mating in litters of three to eight, averaging five. The young are blind and helpless and nearly naked. They are less than 4 inches long and weigh .9 ounce. Eyes and ears open at about 7 days, and the young leave the nest at 16 days. They are weaned between four and five weeks. The female, or doe, rabbit cares for the young, but they get little attention other than nursing. They usually live 2 years in the wild, but up to 10 in captivity.

New England Cottontail
Silvilagus transitionalis

The New England cottontail appears to be declining in range. It is rare in Vermont, New Hampshire and southern Maine. Its distribution is spotty in Connecticut, Massachusetts and Rhode Island.

Description: The New England cottontail resembles the eastern cottontail. The two species have different coat coloring, but are best told apart by skull examination.

The New England cottontail has a darker back, a reddish buff overlaid with black-tipped guard hairs. The rump is slightly duller than the back. The short, rounded ears are heavily furred. The outer edge of the ear has a broad black stripe. There is usually a black spot between the ears, never a white spot as is often found on the eastern cottontail. Albino New England cottontails have been reported.

Adult females are slightly larger than males. Adults are 14.2 to 18.8 inches long, with a tail 1.2 to 1.9 inches and a hind foot 3.5 to 4 inches. They weigh 1.64 to 2.94 pounds.

Distribution: Besides New England, they are found in New York, New Jersey, eastern Pennsylvania, and along the southern

NEW ENGLAND COTTONTAIL

Appalachian Mountains to Georgia.

Ecology: New England cottontails are found from sea level to above 4,000 feet in the southern Appalachians. Primarily they live in dense, bushy woodlands and pine-spruce areas but have been found in habitats as varied as salt marsh to oak forest. Their enemies are the same as those of the eastern cottontail.

Behavior: New England cottontail behavior is much like that of the eastern cottontail. The New England variety is not as likely to be found in open areas and is less high-strung and wary. In the fall it will have a home range of .5 to 1.8 square acres.

Snowshoe Hare
Lepus americanus

This medium-sized hare has two common names which are descriptive. The first is snowshoe hare, a reference to its over-sized hind feet, designed for easy travel over snow. The second is varying hare, because it changes from a brown summer coat to an all-white winter coat as a protective measure.

Description: The snowshoe hare has moderately large ears, a short tail, and large, strong hind legs. There are five toes on the front feet and four on the hind feet. The soles are densely furred in winter.

The fur is thick and soft. The sexes look alike. In summer they are reddish or yellowish brown washed with black along the back and rump. The top of the head is dark, dusky brown, with a tuft of white hairs forming a blaze. The ears are blackish at the tips. The nape is grayish brown; chin, throat and abdomen are usually bright buff to roan. In fall the animals begin converting to all white hair that is gray underneath. The ear tips remain black. Black and albino snowshoe hares occur occasionally.

The autumn molt begins in September or early October and ends in December. The spring molt begins in March and ends by early June.

Females are slightly larger than males. Adults are from 18.3 to 20.3 inches long with a tail 1.4 to 2.0 inches long; the hind foot

will be 5.3 to 5.7 inches long. They weigh 3.1 to 4.4 pounds.

Distribution: They range from Alaska to Newfoundland and the northern United States borders, south in the Appalachian Mountains to eastern Tennessee and western North Carolina, in the Rocky Mountains to New Mexico, and the Sierra Nevada in California.

Ecology: Snowshoe hares live in practically all kinds of forests with brushy ground cover, from near sea level to over 4,000 feet. They prefer mixed hardwood-softwood forest, evergreen swamps, young fir thickets, cut-over areas, second growth birch-poplar, spruce-pine forests, and old burns. They usually avoid open areas.

Snowshoe hares seek shelter in a "form," which may be a knoll or hummock with dry vegetation, the protected side of ledge or rock, clumps of small trees, tree roots, hollow logs or fallen trees. They seldom dig and don't enter holes or burrows. They make beaten runways for travel, especially in swamps.

Man, foxes, Canada lynx, bobcats, martens, fishers, weasels, great horned owls, snowy owls, goshawks, red tailed hawks, and coyotes prey on snowshoe hares. They have ticks, fleas, mites and internal parasites. They are vulnerable to tularemia.

Behavior: Active throughout the year, they move about mostly at twilight and after dark. Occasionally they bask in the sun or

Hoppers and Leapers   57

wallow in dusty places in daylight. They are loners except in breeding season, when several may gather to chase and fight.

In hopping, the front feet are held close together while the hind feet are spread far apart. Snowshoes have been clocked at 31 miles an hour. They have a particular agility that enables them to turn in mid-air. They dislike water but are strong swimmers.

The snowshoe hare will thump its hind feet any time of year, and will make grunting sounds, a low chirping sound, and piercing screams when frightened or hurt. These hares have excellent vision and hearing.

For unknown reasons, they have great population ups and downs; in Maine this is found to follow a 9 to 11 year cycle.

The home range of males is about 25 acres and of females about 19 acres. Males move about more in breeding season. They eat a wide variety of plants. Like cottontail rabbits, they sometimes eat their own feces, apparently to aid in bacterial digestion of their plant food.

In Maine, courtship gets underway in late February, but most snowshoe hares do not breed until March or early April. They produce young from April to August. The young are born 37 days after mating. The young are called leverets and number one to six per litter, averaging three. At birth they are fully furred with their eyes open.

Snowshoe hares are promiscuous and the males will fight fiercely over females and sometimes kill each other. During courtship the male chases the female, and when he catches up she jumps high in the air, often swinging around and landing in another direction.

They are estimated to live to 5 years.

Black-tailed Jackrabbit
Lepus californicus melanotis

The black-tailed jackrabbit owes its presence in New England to the Nantucket Sportsman's Club. The jackrabbit was introduced to Nantucket, off the Massachusetts coast, from Kansas in 1925. These western hares were released on the island as a substitute for the red fox in the traditional "ride to the hounds" by the "Nantucket Harriers." These people rode on horseback dressed

in full English fox hunting regalia and chased the jackrabbits with their hounds. The jackrabbit is now a game animal on Nantucket.

Description: This large hare has enormous ears, a short black tail, powerful hind legs and large feet. The front foot has five toes, the hind foot four. The soles are densely furred.

Scent glands on either side of the anus give off a musky odor, probably used as identification by other hares.

The fur is soft, and males and females look alike with no seasonal changes. The back is grayish to reddish buff with a wavy dark wash of black. The rump has a large whitish patch. A band of broad black runs from the middle of the rump to the top of the tail. There is a whitish ring around the eye and sometimes a small white spot on the forehead. The chin and underparts are whitish. The insides of the ears are buff, the backs whitish and the tips black. Jackrabbits molt in spring and fall.

Hoppers and Leapers   59

Females are larger than males. Adults are 20.1 to 22.8 inches long, with a tail 2 to 4.5 inches long and the hind foot 4.5 to 5.7 inches long. They weigh 5.1 to 7.3 pounds.

Distribution: This is a great plains animal, from southwestern South Dakota and southwestern Wyoming through Colorado and New Mexico east of the Rocky Mountains, all of Kansas, Nebraska, and Oklahoma, western Missouri and Arkansas, and south to north-central Texas.

Ecology: On Nantucket Island jackrabbits have adapted well to beach grass, open fields and cultivated areas along with beach dunes. They scratch out a simple depression as a place to rest or nest. The form is located at the base of large plants which provide overhead cover.

Man is their chief predator. Large birds of prey may capture some of the leverets. They have fleas, ticks, lice and internal parasites.

Behavior: Little is known about their biology on Nantucket. They are alert and skillful in evading capture. They make long, graceful leaps and stride at 35 miles an hour. They are active mainly at dusk and after dark.

Females produce one to three litters a year with one to six young per litter. They are usually born 43 days after mating.

European Hare
Lepus europaeus

This large hare was introduced into Connecticut shortly before 1920, and into Massachusetts in the late 1920's. At present European hares are not found in Massachusetts. It is a game animal hunted in Connecticut's Fairfield and Litchfield counties.

Description: The European hare resembles a larger snowshoe hare, with relatively larger and wider ears, longer and more powerful hind legs.

The fur on the back is wavy and slightly curly. The sexes are the same color. In summer they are rich tawny buff mixed with blackish hairs, paler and yellower on the sides. The neck and shoulders are yellowish buff. The underparts are white and there is a white or buff stripe across the eyes. The ears are grizzled yellow and brownish black, white behind and black at the tips. The tail is black above, white below. The winter coat is paler and grayer, with whitish tones.

Males and females are the same size. They are 25 to 27.3 inches long, with a tail 2.7 to 3.9 inches and a hind foot 6.2 to 6.6. inches. They weigh 7.3 to 10 pounds.

Distribution: European hares were brought to North America for the sport of coursing with hounds. They are found from southern Ontario, Michigan, east to the Hudson River Valley of eastern New York, and in western Connecticut.

Ecology: They prefer open dairy country and low rolling hills with sparse vegetation. Sometimes they are found in open hardwoods with little ground cover.

EUROPEAN HARE

Man, foxes and bobcats are their main predators. Large hawks and owls can catch and hold these creatures, and they are often killed by high-speed farm machines since they have a tendency to freeze as the equipment approaches.

Behavior: European hares are active at twilight and after dark. In the day they rest in forms they scratch out of clumps of grass, weeds or bushes, near boulders or leaf piles. They dig in snow for food and shelter.

They rely on their eyes, ears, and great speed to escape enemies. They have great running endurance. If possible they always start off running uphill. They are good swimmers and don't hesitate to cross rivers. Top speed running is reported to be 30 miles an hour. Their normal stride is four feet, they may leap to 12 feet and can jump over walls five feet high.

They are usually silent, but females emit a faint call to their young, and they scream in fear. The home range is about 11 square miles.

European hares eat grass, clover, corn, winter wheat, apples, blackberries, twigs and buds of thornapple and raspberries, and bark of elm, maple, sumac and butternut trees.

The males fight in breeding season, which starts in early January. As early as mid-March some females are in their second pregnancy. One to three young are born per litter. They probably live to 12 years in the wild.

5. Gnawing Mammals

THE RODENTS, or gnawing mammals, are the largest group of animals, both in species and individuals. These animals characteristically have large front teeth with chisel-like cutting edges.

A greatly varied group, the rodents may live on the ground or in trees; they may glide or spend a lot of time underground, or be largely aquatic water lovers. Most of them are night animals and some are good leapers. Many of them are plant eaters, but some are flesh eaters.

Rodents are important economically, some as valuable fur bearers and others as destructive pests. They are the main food item for many predators.

There are three sub-orders of rodents. They are the sciuromorphs, or squirrel-like rodents; the myomorphs, or rat-like rodents; and hystricomorphs, or porcupine-like rodents. They are distributed worldwide, excepting some arctic and oceanic islands.

Squirrels

Marmots, ground squirrels, prairie dogs, chipmunks, and tree squirrels are in the squirrel family. They typically have bushy tails, and some have cheek pouches. The ground squirrels have shorter legs and less bushy tails. The tree and gliding squirrels are agile and super-active.

Eastern Chipmunk
Tamias striatus

The amount of food a chipmunk can stuff into its cheek pouches is remarkable. They have been recorded as carrying 31 corn kernels and up to 70 sunflower seeds.

Description: The eastern chipmunk is a small, graceful animal, one-third the size of a gray squirrel. The head is short and somewhat rounded with short ears. The tail is flat and not very bushy. The legs are short. The front feet have four clawed toes plus a small thumb covered by a soft, rounded nail. The hind foot has five clawed toes. This small mammal has musk glands on either side of the anus.

The fur is short and dense. Both sexes appear alike. In summer they are reddish brown with a mixture of white and black hairs on the back, blending to bright orange brown or rust on the rump

EASTERN CHIPMUNK

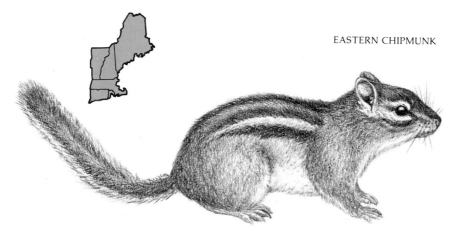

and flanks. The cheeks and body sides are grayish brown to tawny brown. The sides of the face have two buff or whitish stripes above and below the eyes, and a black stripe across the eyes. There are five dark brown to blackish stripes from the shoulders to the rump, separated by white stripes. The belly is white. The feet are buff. The tail is blackish above and rusty below. The coloration of chipmunks is paler in winter. Albino and black chipmunks do occur.

Males and females are the same size, 8.4 to 9.6 inches long with a tail 3 to 4.4 inches long. The hind foot is 1.2 to 1.5 inches. They weigh 2.5 to 3.9 ounces.

Distribution: They live from Quebec south through the eastern half of the United States to Georgia, western Florida, and north-eastern Louisiana, and west to eastern Oklahoma, Kansas, North and South Dakota, and Saskatchewan.

Ecology: The eastern chipmunk is found in the borders of hard-wood forests where thick understory and brier grow among old logs, on rocky ledges covered with brush and vines, on loose stone walls, in old forests without undergrowth, in old farm woodlots, brushland, brushy fencerows, old buildings and some-times parks and gardens.

They rarely climb trees and make dens in burrows which usually have the entrance hidden under an old log, stump, rock or stone wall. In cold weather the den entrance is plugged.

Man, hawks, mink, weasels, martens, foxes, bobcats, house cats, raccoons, Norway rats, red squirrels and large snakes kill them. They have fleas, lice, mites and internal parasites.

Behavior: Chipmunks are daytime animals, more active in spring and fall than summer. Usually they go into their burrows in late October to early November to hibernate lightly, emerging to breed in late February or early March, but they may become inactive again before spring.

They make three sounds: a loud "chip" similar to a robin's note, a soft "cuck-cuck" note they may repeat for several minutes, and a combination of a loud chip with a trill on the end—like, "chip-r-r-r-r."

Normally chipmunks are solitary, except for females with young. The biggest chipmunks seem to be the most aggressive against the smaller. They have a home range of about .37 acres for males and .26 for females. Their territories often overlap, and each animal defends ground centered on the entrance to its burrow.

Chipmunks feed on nuts and a wide variety of seeds. They also eat mushrooms, berries, cherries, corn, sunflower seeds, watermelon, apples, pears, peaches, cantaloupe, and squash. Insects, earthworms, small moles, mice, sparrows, juncos, eggs, frogs and snakes are among the animal items they eat.

They breed in spring and summer. The young are born 31 days after mating, one to eight per litter. Females may have two litters a year. At birth they are red, naked and blind. The eyes open in 30 to 31 days, and the young shed their milk teeth at 3 months. They live 2 to 3 years in the wild.

Woodchuck
Marmota monax

Woodchucks have a perpetual weight problem. They spend six months of the year gaining it, and six months losing it as they alternate between a long hibernation and active periods.

Description: The largest member of the squirrel family in New England, woodchucks are generally fat with short, powerful legs and a short, bushy tail. The ears are low and round and can be closed to keep out dirt. Each front foot has four toes with strong claws and a small thumb with a small nail. The hind feet have five strong toes with claws. There are three white glands located just within the anus which give off a musky odor.

Males and females look alike. Their coloration varies greatly but they are generally grizzled brown above with a cinnamon cast. The tops of the head, face, legs, and tail are dark brown. The sides of the nose, chin and lips are buff-white. The underparts are buff. White or black woodchucks occur. They molt in spring.

Males are slightly larger than females. Adults measure 17.6 to 24.6 inches, with a tail 3.9 to 6.1 inches long. The hind foot averages between 2.7 to 3.4 inches. Weights vary seasonally from 6.2 pounds to 10 pounds, with some woodchucks weighing up to 15 pounds.

Distribution: Woodchucks are found from Labrador and Nova Scotia south to the northern parts of Georgia, Alabama, and Northwestern Louisiana, west to eastern Kansas, and north-westward into Alaska.

Ecology: Woodchucks prefer edges of brushy woodlands and high, rolling fields. They may be found along stream banks, near roads and railroads, and sometimes near barns or other buildings.

Woodchucks are ground dwellers and build simple and complex burrows. They may go down 6 feet or more in loose, sandy soil, or 2 to 4 feet in gravelly ground. The burrow may be 10 to 40 feet long, often with several blind pockets where the woodchuck defecates. Usually burrows have a 15 inch diameter hibernation chamber and a nesting chamber lined with leaves and grass. Sometimes there is a winter den located in a wooded area which will have only one or two entrances. The summer den in an open area has a main entrance marked by a dirt pile, and a less noticeable escape hole, well hidden in vegetation.

Man, dogs, foxes, black bears, large hawks, owls, bobcats, mink, weasels and large rattlesnakes kill woodchucks. They have fleas, mites, ticks and internal parasites and are subject to tularemia, rabies and other diseases. Flooding sometimes drowns the young and hibernating woodchucks. Any malformation of the incisor teeth may result in starvation, since the animal can't cut its food off. The tooth may continue to grow and may even penetrate the skull.

Behavior: Though woodchucks are usually solitary, small groups may gather for feeding or sunning. Their home range depends on how close food is to their den. In a clover or alfalfa field it might be as little as 20 yards.

Woodchucks aren't very smart. They never seem to learn to avoid traps, even when repeatedly caught, but they are strong and fierce fighters when cornered. When frightened they can run about 10 miles an hour for short distances.

They will give a shrill whistle or an alarm call, preceded by a low, abrupt "phew" and often followed by a sound like "tchuck, tchuck." They will grind their teeth loudly when angry or scared. Happy woodchucks in captivity grunt or purr softly.

Woodchucks are clean animals. They deposit their wastes in pockets off the main burrow or bury them in the entrance mound. Most of their time is spent resting or sleeping in the den. They are

WOODCHUCK

mostly daytime animals.

Woodchucks don't store food. They eat voraciously as summer advances on a wide variety of succulent plants, gaining body fat.

They are deep hibernators and, while they are not easily awakened, they sometimes emerge from their burrows during warm spells in winter.

While they are ground animals, they are also pretty good climbers and easily climb 15 feet or more up trees to escape enemies, to get at fruit, or just to enjoy the view. They enjoy sunbathing on elevated locations, and they are strong swimmers.

They mate from early March to late April. The young are born 32 days after mating in litters of two to eight. They are born blind, naked and helpless, colored dark pink. The young nurse for about 44 days. At 5 weeks old they emerge from the burrow to romp and feed. Woodchucks probably live 3 to 4 years in the wild.

WILD MAMMALS OF NEW ENGLAND

Gray Squirrel
Sciurus carolinensis pennsylvanicus

Alert, nervous and wily in the wild, the gray squirrel is also one of the friendliest creatures when found in city parks. Sometimes it can be coaxed into taking food from a hand.

Description: This slender tree squirrel has a broad, flattened tail of about half its body length. The hind legs are much larger than the front ones, an adaptation for leaping. Males and females look alike.

In summer the upper parts are yellowish brown, slightly grayish on the sides of the neck, shoulders and thighs. The face is cinnamon-buff, forelegs gray above, hind legs reddish, and the tail is brown at the base, banded with black and tan broadly tipped with white. The chin, throat and underparts are whitish. There is a white-buff ring around the eye and white on the backs of the ears. The winter fur is more grayish, and is heavily frosted with white-tipped hairs.

Color phases include blacks, reds, albinos and blendings of red and blacks. Molts take place in the spring and fall.

Males and females are the same size, 17.9 to 20.7 inches long, with tail 6.4 to 9.8 inches and the hind foot 2.3 to 2.9 inches. They weigh from 12 to 24 ounces.

Distribution: Gray squirrels are found in forested areas from southern Quebec, New Brunswick, and Ontario to Florida, west into eastern Texas, and north into southern Manitoba. They have been introduced in Washington, British Columbia, and Vancouver Island.

Ecology: They live in hardwood, and hardwood-softwood, forests, particularly where there are nut-producing oaks, beeches, hickories, butternuts, and black walnuts; also in small woodlots, farm woodlands, city parks and wooded residential areas.

Using tree cavities for permanent homes, they use leaf nests for temporary shelter. These bulky, round nests are firmly woven of small twigs and leaves with the inside lined with shredded bark, moss, grass, ferns, paper, cloth and other soft materials. A nest may weigh 7 pounds and have an outside diameter of 12 to 14 inches.

Man, foxes, raccoons, bobcats, house cats, hawks, owls and pilot black snakes eat gray squirrels. They are infested by fleas, lice, and ticks, and may suffer from scabies, mange, rabies, tetanus and internal parasites.

Behavior: They have keen senses of smell, hearing, sight and touch. They are most active at dawn and late afternoon and spend most of the day in a nest or resting on a limb. They don't hibernate, but will stay in the nest during extreme cold or stormy weather.

They are tree dwellers but come to the ground to feed. They can run 10 miles an hour for short distances and leap 10 feet. They are strong swimmers.

Included among their calls are those used for apprehension, fright, after feeding, fussing, a variety of clucking calls and a death squeal.

Gray squirrels are somewhat social animals, but a female will defend her den tree against other females when she has young. They are homebodies with a territory that is not much over an acre. They have been known to have mass migrations from their home areas in the fall for unexplained reasons.

GRAY SQUIRREL

Their feeding sites are often marked with gnawed shells, twig clippings and dislodged fruits. They commonly cache acorns and other nuts for winter use.

Gray squirrels eat acorns and other nuts, buds, the inner bark of trees, cherries, grapes, apples, mushrooms, and corn. Sometimes they eat insects, young birds and eggs, and they gnaw on antlers, bones and turtle shells.

Promiscuous breeders, they mate during midwinter and sometimes in May and June. They give birth about 44 days after mating, with one to nine in a litter. The young are born blind and helpless. The eyes open at 4 to 5 weeks, and they are weaned between 8 and 10 weeks. The spring litter usually remains with the female until she has a second litter; the second litter usually stays with her through the winter. Females live at least 12½ years in the wild; males live about 9 years.

Red Squirrel
Tamiasciurus hudsonicus

Pugnacious is the word for the red squirrel. It is aggressive and unsociable and will defend food and home territory against birds and other squirrels.

Description: Half the size of a gray squirrel, the red squirrel has a tail almost as long as its head and body, though rather narrow for that of a tree squirrel. There are four toes on each front foot and five on each hind foot.

Males and females look alike. In summer they are rusty reddish gray with black markings above, the sides olive-gray with the legs, feet, tail and ears reddish. The lips, chin, throat, belly, inner limbs and a ring around the eye are whitish or faintly yellowish. There is a narrow or wide black lateral stripe extending along the sides, separating the reddish upper part from the whitish belly. The tail is reddish above and yellowish gray to dull rust below.

In winter the color above is chestnut, blending to olive-gray on the sides, slightly flecked with black, and the lateral stripes nearly or completely faded out. Red squirrels molt in spring and winter.

Males and females are the same size, 10.9 to 13.7 inches long, with a tail 4.4 to 5.9 inches and the hind foot 1.8 to 2 inches. They weigh 5.8 to 8.4 ounces.

Distribution: Red squirrels are transcontinental, found from Alaska to northern Quebec, south to South Carolina and Tennessee in the Appalachian Mountains, and in the Rockies to New Mexico, Arizona, and across California into British Columbia.

Ecology: This squirrel prefers evergreen forests of deep spruce, hemlock, pine and balsam, and to a lesser degree hardwoods; it is found in barns and deserted buildings in wooded areas.

It nests among branches against a tree trunk, in tree cavities, crows' and hawks' nests, and sometimes in stone walls or burrows. The bulky nest exterior is made of cones, leaves, and twigs. The inner lining is of shredded bark, moss, dried leaves and grass. The outside is 10 to 20 inches in diameter with an inner chamber 3 to 6 inches. The nest is often 5 feet from the top of the tree and as much as 65 feet above ground.

Man, martens, fishers, mink, bobcats, house cats, foxes, weasels, large hawks, owls and tree climbing snakes feed on red squirrels. Pickerel, pike and snapping turtles sometimes get them while they swim. They have fleas, ticks, mites and internal parasites but appear free of disease, although they might get tularemia and rabies.

Behavior: Active mostly between dawn and dusk, red squirrels sometimes are heard at night. They are about all year long except during stormy weather.

Mainly tree dwellers, they spend a lot of time on the ground and sometimes burrow in soft soil, making nesting chambers and underground food storerooms.

Red squirrels have two kinds of territories: defended winter food caches which are abandoned in summer, and specific areas defended year round.

They are noisy and often stamp their feet in anger, their tails jerking furiously while they angrily chatter "chir-r-r-r, chir-r-r-r." At times they just chatter cheerfully and may spend hours spread out on a limb in rest. Sometimes they are seen chasing each other about in obvious play, but this usually involves litter mates.

Red squirrels are agile in the trees and can leap 5 feet with a

RED SQUIRREL

rise of 3 feet. They can fall considerable distances without harm and can run about 14 miles an hour. Strong swimmers, they readily take to water.

Unlike gray squirrels, they do not store their food at random, but bury it in large underground caches containing a bushel or more.

Red squirrels eat the seeds of various pines, larches, spruce, fir, hemlock and cedar. They will eat almost any kind of nut, and their diet includes seeds, berries, buds, tender leaves, inner bark and flowering parts of many kinds of trees, a variety of berries and cherries. They relish maple sap in spring and will strip limb bark to get it. They also eat grasses, mushrooms, insects, snails, birds and their eggs, and they may kill young rabbits and gray squirrels.

Breeding season is from mid-January to late September. Usually there are two litters a year. Red squirrels are promiscuous. The young are born 36 to 40 days after mating, from 1 to 7 per litter.

The young are born pink, naked, blind and helpless. They develop slowly, becoming fully furred at about 1 month. They live 2 years or longer.

Gnawing Mammals   73

Southern Flying Squirrel

Glaucomys volans

Flying squirrels don't. They glide. They volplane through the air like a soaring glider from tree to tree. They launch themselves with legs outspread, extending a membrane, and can go 150 feet or more from a height of 60 feet.

Description: The southern flying squirrel has a loose fold of skin fully furred on both sides which extends from the outside of the wrist in the front leg to the ankle on the hind leg. It also has a broad, flat tail with a rounded tip. The gliding membrane is supported by a spur of cartilage at the wrist which allows it to be extended beyond the outstretched wrist. The membrane lies in loose folds when the squirrel is resting or running, but when it jumps into space the membrane is stretched out and acts like a parachute, with the tail as a rudder-stabilizer.

The head is blunt and round and the eyes large and dark. The ears are large and the whiskers long. While the legs are long, the feet are small. The front foot has four toes and the hind foot has five.

The fur is soft, dense and long. Males and females look alike. In winter the color above is drab to pinkish cinnamon or fawn brown. The sides are darker, almost black along the side of the membrane. The underparts are white or tinged creamy white. The head is grayish or buff and the ears are light brown. The tail is brownish gray above and light pinkish cinnamon below. The feet are gray above and whitish below. The toes are white. These squirrels are darker in summer. There is one molt a year in the fall.

Males and females are the same size, 8.2 to 10 inches long, with a tail 3.1 to 4.3 inches and the hind foot 1 to 1.4 inches. They weigh 1.8 to 2.5 ounces.

Distribution: These squirrels are found from Nova Scotia, southern Ontario, central Minnesota, Wisconsin, Michigan, and northern New York south to southern Florida, the northern Gulf Coast, eastern Texas, northern Arkansas and Oklahoma, and west to eastern Nebraska and Kansas.

Ecology: Southern flying squirrels live in mature hardwoods,

SOUTHERN FLYING SQUIRREL

usually near water. They prefer red maple, oak, aspen, beech, walnut, and birch, with an abundance of nuts. They are also found in mixed hardwood-softwoods (including old orchards), in attics, lofts, or under eaves. They prefer old woodpecker nests for shelter, but may build a nest in a hole in snags, stubs or hollow limbs. Once in a while they will live in a bird house.

Man, bobcats, house cats, foxes, weasels, great horned owls and tree climbing snakes are among their enemies. They have lice, mites, chiggers and interior parasites.

Behavior: The females sometimes carry their young while gliding. When they mistakenly land in water they are poor swimmers, and they are nearly helpless in high grass.

Southern flying squirrels are active all night and rarely seen in daylight. They are sociable and active all year, although during cold weather they may become inactive and then several will snuggle together in a nest for warmth.

Southern flying squirrels are delicate, gentle and shy. A slight wound or rough handling may kill them. They rarely attempt to bite when caught. They make a sound like a weak bird chirp when feeding, but get louder and may stamp their feet when angry. Females seem to have a territory of about an acre; the territory is about one-third more for males.

Males don't appear to be territorial, but females will defend their entire home range.

They eat a host of plant materials including seeds, nuts, berries, buds, blossoms, maple sap, corn and mushrooms. They also eat moths, beetles, insects, birds and their eggs.

Flying squirrels have two mating seasons, one in February through March and another from June through July. The young are born 40 days after mating, two to six per litter.

The young are born blind, naked and helpless. About 2.4 inches long at birth, they double their size in a week. At 28 days they are well-furred with the eyes open, and they are weaned shortly after 5 weeks. They probably live to 5 years in the wild.

Northern Flying Squirrel
Glaucomys sabrinus macrotis

Northern flying squirrels are gentle, sociable and gregarious in winter.

Description: They resemble the southern flying squirrel but are larger, darker and redder above. The white hairs on the belly are slate at the base instead of pure white.

Males and females are the same size, 9.8 to 11.5 inches long, with a tail 4.5 to 5.3 inches and a hind foot 1.4 to 1.6 inches. They weigh from 2 to 4.4 ounces.

Distribution: Northern flying squirrels are found from southeastern Alaska across northern Canada; south through most of New England to western Pennsylvania; south into the Appalachian Mountains to North Carolina and eastern Tennessee; west to eastern North Dakota; in the Rocky Mountains south into Utah; along the Pacific coast, south to northern California; and from western California south into western Nevada and the San Bernadino Mountains.

Ecology: They are found at altitudes of 1,000 feet or more in cool mixed forests of hard and softwoods, favoring stands of hemlock-birch or hemlock-maple.

The nest is usually in a natural tree cavity or an old woodpecker hole. Occasionally, these squirrels build a nest in an

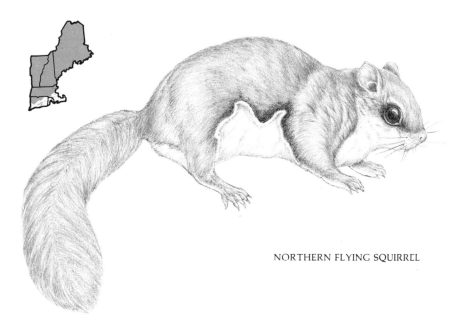

NORTHERN FLYING SQUIRREL

abandoned building or may use abandoned squirrel or crows' nests. In summer they use an outside nest built close to a tree trunk 5 to 30 feet above ground. The outside of the nest is made of strips of bark and twigs, and the interior is lined with shredded bark, grass and other soft plants.

Their enemies include man, bobcats, house cats, martens, fishers, weasels, great horned owls and tree-climbing snakes. They have fleas, mice, chiggers and internal parasites.

Behavior: Their general behavior is thought to be like the southern flying squirrel's. They have a somewhat softer and lower voice and are active on the snow to temperatures at least as low as 10°F. Sometimes they make tunnels in the snow similar to those made by weasels.

They eat nuts, seeds, buds, catkins, berries, fruits, insects, slugs, small birds and their eggs, small mammals, lichens and mushrooms.

They seem to have two litters a year, one in late March to early July and the other in late August or September. The young are born about 37 days after mating with a litter of two to six.

Beavers

Beavers are huge rodents, exceeded in size only by the capybara of Panama and South America. Their large, flat, scaly tails make them easily recognizable. There is only one species found in New England.

Beavers are found throughout North America, excepting parts of northern Alaska and northern Canada, central Nevada, parts of California, western Utah, Florida and most of Mexico.

Beaver

Castor canadensis

Busy as a beaver is a trite saying, but nonetheless accurate. Cutting trees, building and repairing dams, making lodges, and cutting canals and burrows all keep the beaver moving.

Stories about beaver industriousness and intelligence are legion, and generally overdone. One such story says a beaver can fell a tree in any direction it wants. The truth is, the trees fall pretty much where they may, sometimes even landing on the beaver fatally.

BEAVER

WILD MAMMALS OF NEW ENGLAND

Description: Compact and heavy-bodied, beaver have powerful muscles. Each foot has five clawed toes. The tail is flat, broad, nearly hairless and scaled. The head is small and rounded. The nose, ears, and mouth all close automatically when the beaver dives. The front incisor teeth are like wood chisels. The front feet are like hands and not webbed but have claws for carrying and digging. When the beaver swims it holds its fore-paws close to its body. The hind feet are large and webbed. The two inner toes on the hind feet are cleft for combing the fur and for spreading oil which is obtained from two abdominal oil glands. In addition, the beaver has two much larger castor, or anal, scent glands; these produce a pungent yellow-brown oil which is deposited on scent mounds made of mud. These scent posts are up to 2 feet high.

The tail is used as a rudder and sculling oar. It also helps regulate body temperature, stores body fats, acts as balance for standing up, and is used for warning when the beaver slaps it loudly on water.

The fur is dense, short and soft. The underfur is waterproof and the guard hairs are sparse, long and shiny. Telling male and female beaver apart is a job for experts—both sexes are rich brownish black or yellowish brown above and paler below. Ears, feet and tail are blackish. White, black and silver beaver have been reported.

Males and females are about the same size, 32 to 48.1 inches long with a tail 12 to 20.5 inches and a hind foot 5/5 to 7.5 inches long. They weigh 27 to 67 pounds.

Distribution: Beaver once ranged most of the regions of North America, from Alaska across most of Canada and south to central California, northern Nevada, northern Mexico, the Gulf coastal plain, and extreme northern Florida. The species was exterminated in many areas and was later reintroduced to some sections.

Ecology: Gently sloping streams, rivers and quiet lakes, and marshes bordered by stands of small timber such as aspen, birch, poplar, maple and willow are home for the beaver.

Dams are their most impressive works; these create water depth to float food and building materials to the lodge and furnish protection from land predators. Working from upstream, beavers lay sticks, leaves, grass, sod and mud across a stream until the flow is checked. Then they push sticks over the top and allow them to crisscross on the low slope until the dam is high enough and strong enough to hold the desired amount of water. The average height of a beaver dam is 2½ to 3 feet, but they get to 10 feet and 200 or more feet long.

The beaver lodge is usually surrounded by water but may be built against a bank. Roughly conical, the lodge may be up to 8 feet high above water and 40 feet wide. The floor is semi-dry and clean of droppings, usually bedded with grass, sedges, moss or shredded wood. The walls are usually 2 to 3 feet thick at the bottom and much thinner and looser at the top, where an opening provides ventilation. Trappers call the top opening of a lodge the "smoke hole."

Beavers may build bank burrows along large, swift streams where building a dam or lodge would be difficult. They build canals to float logs to a pond, and they also build canals in shallow ponds to widen and deepen them. On land beavers create trails as they repeatedly use the same route.

Beaver scent mounds are located at the water's edge to establish home territory. Beavers seem to maintain separate territories between colonies with no overlap.

Man, black bears, coyotes, foxes, dogs, Canada lynxes, bobcats and probably fishers prey on beaver. Large hawks and owls may take the unwary kits, or young, on land. Beaver have screwworms and tiny bloodsucking beetles, along with internal parasites, and suffer from tularemia, rabies, lung fungus, and lumpy jaw.

Behavior: Beavers live in colonies of up to 12 members, consisting of a male and female along with their yearlings and kits. The adult female usually is dominant.

Active throughout the year, beavers are mostly nocturnal. They spend most of their time feeding, doing the most eating in the first half of the night. They don't like hard rain and may go into the lodge to avoid it.

They are slow but graceful swimmers at about 2 miles an hour. They can stay submerged for up to 15 minutes. Under the ice they get oxygen from air bubbles and air holes. On land they walk with a slow shuffle but can run about as fast as a person.

A beaver will cut an average of one tree every two days, aspen or cottonwood taking much less time than oak or birch. Once a small tree is felled, several beaver may feed on the bark. They gnaw off sections in 3 to 6 foot lengths, which they drag to the water. Usually they will go no more than 300 feet from water to cut a tree.

In early autumn they begin to build an underwater food cache by piling up green branches and logs in some deep part of the pond near the lodge. Food caches are 3 to 10 feet high and 20 to 40 feet in diameter. Their food preference is hardwood bark, but they eat plants and grasses.

Beavers appear to mate for life, although the male may mate with other females. The breeding season is mid-January to mid-March. Kits are born about 106 days after mating in litters of 1 to 9. They are born fully furred and with their eyes open. At 2 to 3 weeks they start eating vegetation, and they are weaned by the time they are 6 weeks old. They may stay with their parents for 2 years. They have lived to 20 years in captivity.

Mice and Rats

The family Cricetidae is made up of New World mice, rats, voles, hamsters, lemmings and the related species. They are the largest in terms of number of species. They are found in a wide variety of habitats from desert to rain forest to tundra.

There are two subfamilies in the grouping. The first are the cricetine rodents with slender to robust bodies, pointed muzzles and long tails. The other is the microtines which are stocky and robust, with blunt muzzles and short tails.

Deer Mouse
Peromyscus maniculatus

In captivity a deer mouse might live to be 8 years old, but in the wild it is doing well to see its first birthday.

Description: The deer mouse and white-footed mouse are similar in appearance. The deer mouse has soft grayish fur with only a slight mid-back stripe. The tail is usually as long or longer than the head and body. The ears are medium-sized and thinly haired. The black eyes are prominent. There are four clawed toes and tiny nailed thumb on the front foot and five clawed toes on the hind foot. They have small cheek pouches. The tail is hairy, with scales and a long tuft of hairs on the end, and can grasp objects to a limited degree.

Males and females are the same color, rich brownish gray mixed with darker hairs along the middle of the back from the shoulders to the tail. The ears are dusky, edged with gray. The tail is brownish black above and white below. These mice have a single annual molt which starts in June and ends in late summer.

Males and females are the same size, 6.8 to 8.4 inches long with a tail 3.1 to 4.1 inches. They weigh .56 to .98 ounce.

Distribution: Deer mice are found from Alaska across Canada, south in the Appalachians to northern Georgia, west through Tennessee, Arkansas, southward to central Mexico and Baja

California, and northward along the Pacific coast.

In New England they are found from northern Maine to the Berkshires in western Massachusetts and northwestern Connecticut. Deer mice do not occur naturally in the coastal plains of southernmost Maine, eastern Massachusetts, Connecticut or Rhode Island.

Ecology: Deer mice prefer forests of white, red and black spruce and balsam fir, or northern hardwoods of beech, sugar maple and yellow birch. They are found along fencerows, field borders, and places where trees are small and ground cover dense. Their nests are in stone walls, old cabins, farm buildings, tree roots and stumps, hollow logs, granaries, corn shocks, under rocks and boards, abandoned burrows and bird nests. The nest is made of grass, leaves and other plant material and is lined with shredded plants, hair, feathers, cotton, rags and other soft materials.

Man, foxes, house cats, weasels, mink, short-tailed shrews, hawks, owls and snakes prey on them. Fleas, ticks, chiggers, mites, botfly larvae and internal parasites infest them.

Behavior: Active throughout the year except in the worst winter weather, deer mice are mostly night animals. They have well-developed senses of hearing, smell, taste and vision. They are capable tree climbers and strong swimmers, although they don't like water. Generally calm, they stamp their feet when disturbed. They make high squeaks and a shrill buzzing sound.

In autumn they cache ripe seeds, mast and other nuts in hollow trees, logs, stumps, nests and burrows near their nest chambers. Deer mice eat a wide variety of seeds, berries, nuts and grains, also small fruits, mushrooms, grubs, larvae, worms, snails, caterpillars, and sometimes dead animals.

The breeding season starts in March and extends through October. The young are born about 23 days after mating in litters of three to seven. A female may give birth four times in a year. The newborn are blind, naked, and pinkish, and very vocal. They are weaned by 4 weeks. Both parents live in the nest with the young, and the male may even assist in their care.

White-footed Mouse
Peromyscus leucopus

White-footed mice prefer to nest in trees above ground level near the edge of woods, although they may make a home on the ground when there is snow cover.

Description: Males and females look alike, their backs a rich reddish brown, darker on the middle of the back. The underparts and feet are white. In appearance they look much like deer mice.

They are 6.1 to 7.4 inches long with a tail 2.4 to 3.4 inches long. They weigh .56 to 1.02 an ounce.

Distribution: White-footed mice are found in forests and brush in the eastern United States north of a line drawn from southeastern Mississippi to northeastern North Carolina, west to western Montana and eastern Arizona, and south through eastern Mexico to Yucatan. In New England they are found in all but northernmost Maine.

Ecology: They are primarily shrubland and woodland inhabitants, preferring drier areas than the deer mouse in hemlocks, white pine and oaks.

White-footed mice may build nests in stone walls, in ledges, under old stumps and logs, in hollow trees, under a board or slab, in corn shocks, beehives or old squirrel and bird's nests. The globular nest is 8 to 12 inches in diameter, made of dried grasses, leaves, moss and plant materials, and lined with lichens, milkweed, shredded grass, cedar bark, hair and feathers. A pair of mice may build two or more nests. They often leave scats in their nests. They have the same predators and parasites as the deer mouse.

Behavior: Active dusk to dawn, year round (except in the worst of winter), they are social, and two or more may live together. They are good swimmers.

White-footed mice feed on hemlock seeds, acorns, small fruit, clover, insects, grubs, larvae, caterpillars, small dead birds and dead mice. They cache food for future use and are estimated to eat 30 percent of their weight each day.

The breeding season is from late February into November. The

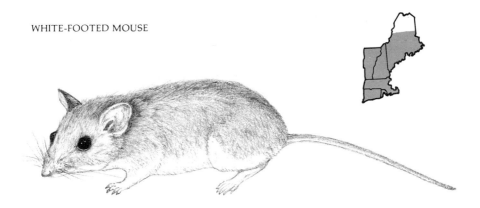

young are born 22 to 25 days after mating, with three to seven per litter. The newborn are blind, helpless and pink, weighing about .07 ounce. They are sexually mature at 7 to 8 weeks old.

Gapper's Red-backed Mouse
Clethrionomys gapperi

Irritable and nervous, red-backed mice will fight when placed together. When bothered they give a shrill chattering.

Description: A short tail and reddish color set this species off from most other mice in New England. It looks like a pine vole but has only red on its back, and has larger ears and a longer tail than the vole. Its fur is also longer, coarser.

The front feet have four toes, the hind feet five toes. Males and females look alike. In winter there is a broad stripe of bright chestnut, sprinkled with black hairs, from the forehead to the base of the tail, contrasting with the reddish buff of the nose and sides of the head and body. The underparts are pale buff to silvery. The feet are gray, the tail brownish above and white below, tufted at the tip. In summer they are slightly darker and duller.

Males and females are the same size, 4.9 to 6 inches long with a tail 1.2 to 2 inches long. They weigh .56 to 1.12 ounces.

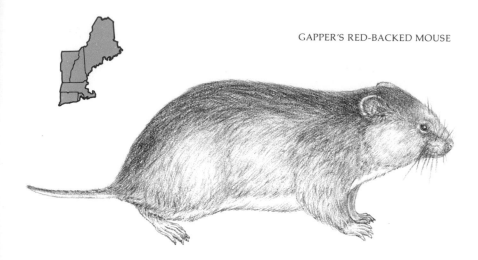

Distribution: This mouse is found across Canada south into the Appalachians to western North Carolina, in northern Michigan, most of Wisconsin, Minnesota, and North Dakota, through the Rocky Mountains, and south to southwestern New Mexico.

Ecology: A woodland mouse, it is found in cool hemlock and red spruce forests, preferring damp areas strewn with mossy rocks, stumps, rotten logs, and root systems in loose forest litter, it is also at home in sphagnum or fern-filled depressions or around old white cedar swamps with sparse to medium cover.

Most often, red-backed mice live in mole, vole and other small mammal burrows. The nest, which is about 4 inches in diameter, is made of dry grass, leaves, bark, twigs and hemlock cones. It may be found among the roots of small trees, or on top of the ground under a stump root. The mice make burrows that often come to the surface.

Man, birds of prey, coyotes, foxes, skunks, weasels, mink, opossums, cats and snakes prey on them. They have fleas, ticks and internal parasites.

Behavior: Red-backed mice are active all year, at all hours, but more so at night. They can jump to 8 inches and are agile climbers. They are fairly good swimmers. Their estimated home range is 3.56 acres.

They feed on the leaves and tender stems of many weeds and grasses, seeds, berries, nuts, roots, buds, ferns and fungi, along with insects, spiders and snails. During severe winter weather they eat seeds and tubers cached in burrows.

Breeding season begins in mid-January and lasts well into November. The young are born 17 to 19 days after mating in litters of two to eight. The newborn are blind and hairless and weigh about .07 ounce. Their eyes open in 13 days and they are weaned at 17 days. There may be three litters a year.

Meadow Vole
Microtus pennsylvanicus

Not often noticed, the meadow vole is one of the most abundant mammals in New England. It lives in extensive, complex underground tunnels, and pathways in dense grass and other growth, and is seldom seen.

Description: Thick-bodied, the meadow vole has a short, scaly, scantily haired tail about twice as long as its hind foot. The eyes are beady and black. The ears are short, rounded, and furred along the borders. The meadow vole looks like the pine vole but has larger ears, a longer tail and coarser fur.

Males and females look alike. In summer they are dull chestnut brown or yellowish brown on the back. The underparts are grayish white or buffy white. The feet are grayish brown. The tail is dusky above and paler below. In winter, their coats are

MEADOW VOLE

grayer. All-white, white-spotted, albino, black, yellow and cinnamon meadow voles are reported.

Males are slightly larger than females. Adults are 5.9 to 7.6 inches long with a tail 1.3 to 2.5 inches long. They weigh from .70 to 2.28 ounces.

Distribution: Meadow voles are found from Quebec and New Brunswick south into Georgia and west into Nebraska, South Dakota, and North Dakota.

Ecology: They are found in grass-sedge marshes, salt marshes, wooded swamps, sphagnum bogs, along streams and lakes, in orchards, open woodland, corn shocks, haystacks, and other grain cover.

The meadow vole makes a round nest, up to 8 inches in diameter, from dried vegetation. It may be located in a grass tussock, a runway, or underground. The winter underground nest is smaller.

Man, hawks, owls, crows, jays, gulls, herons, shrikes, house cats, bobcats, lynxes, raccoons, mink, weasels, dogs, foxes, skunks, opossums, short-tailed shrews, bears, bass, pickerel and snakes prey on meadow voles. They have fleas, mites, and internal parasites. Some inherit the trait called "waltzing" in which they circle rapidly left or right with jerky head movements.

Behavior: Meadow voles are gregarious, fierce and aggressive. They are active all year, day and night. They can run up to 5 miles an hour. They are good swimmers and can dive.

Meadow voles defend a home territory and seldom travel from it.

They mainly eat grass, sedges, legumes, seeds, grains, tubers and roots. They eat bark and will often girdle a young tree. Sometimes they store food. They will eat meat when it is available.

Among the most prolific of mammals, the meadow vole is promiscuous. A female can produce 17 litters a year. The number of litters depends on food availability. Meadow voles will breed throughout the year when food is available. The young are born about 21 days after mating in litters of one to nine. They are blind, pink and helpless at birth; by the third week they are independent. Females become sexually mature at 4 weeks old. Meadow voles live less than a year in the wild.

Beach Vole
Microtus breweri

The beach vole is found only on Muskeget Island, located off the west coast of Nantucket Island, off the southern coast of Massachusetts.

Description: Closely related to the meadow vole, the beach vole is larger, with a shorter tail and paler, coarser fur. Males and females look alike. The fur is pale or light gray sprinkled with longer black hairs on the back and sides. The belly is whitish and the feet gray or grayish white. The tail is whitish below, brownish above. There is usually a white blaze on the forehead, and sometimes on the chin and throat.
   They range in size from 6.8 to 8.4 inches long, with a tail 1.6 to 2.3 inches long.

Ecology: Beach voles construct frail nests anywhere on loose soil or under some shelter. Usually large enough to hold just one animal, the typical nest is open on top and made of fine grass. Nests for bearing young are built under stalks of beach goldenrod or a fragment of wood, or in a short nesting burrow.
   They are preyed upon by house cats, short-eared owls and marsh hawks. Much of their habitat has been destroyed by erosion after hurricanes and by construction on the 1.2-mile-long island.

Behavior: Beach voles seek cover among the sparse beach growth, driftwood, and wreckage. They are adapted for digging in sand and make extensive runways through beach grass. Their primary food is beach grass, and in autumn they store it for winter use by burying it in sand.

Not much is known about beach vole reproduction. They probably have litters throughout the warm months, with four to five young per litter.

Rock Vole
Microtus chrotorrhinus

The rock vole prefers to live at high elevations, generally over 3,000 feet; on Mount Washington, it is found at 5,300 feet.

Description: This variety looks much like the meadow vole, but has a yellow-orange nose and yellowish color below the ears and rump.

Males and females are the same size, 5.5 to 6.9 inches long with a tail 1.8 to 2 inches long. They weigh 1.05 to 1.40 ounces.

Distribution: Rock voles are found from Labrador, eastern Quebec, northern New Brunswick, and central Ontario west to the east side of Lake Superior and northeastern Minnesota, and from Maine, New Hampshire and Vermont into the Adirondacks and Catskills in New York and Pennsylvania, southward along

ROCK VOLE

the crest of the Appalachians into North Carolina, Tennessee and probably Kentucky.

Ecology: They prefer deep, cool, damp crevices along streams among moss-covered rocks in areas with growths of spruce and fir.

Man, short-tailed shrews, and bobcats prey on them. They have fleas and internal parasites.

Behavior: Rock voles do not appear to hibernate, even in the most severe winter weather. They are daytime animals, most active in morning.

Rock voles cut plant leaves and carry them between rocks or under logs to eat. Alpine goldenrods, mountain avens, bunchberry, blackberry, false miterwort, mayflower, violet, mosses and grasses are among their food items.

They breed from late March to mid-October, producing up to three litters a year. There are one to seven young per litter.

Pine Vole
Microtus pinetorum scalopsoides

The pine vole is the most dedicated digger among the members of this family, making burrows in loose, well-drained soil and seldom leaving its protection.

Description: Looking like the meadow vole, the pine vole has a shorter tail and ears, and velvety russet fur. The front feet are enlarged for digging, and each has four toes and a small thumb. The hind foot has five toes. Breeding males have prominent anal glands.

Males and females look alike. The back is bright chestnut and the underparts are slate or silvery gray. The back and rump occasionally have silver-tipped hairs. The tail is brownish above and paler below. The feet are brownish gray. Buff, white-spotted, cream, orange-yellow and albino pine voles have been reported.

They range from 4.3 to 5.3 inches long, with a tail .59 to 1.01 inches long. They weigh .70 to 1.30 ounces.

Distribution: Pine voles are found from north central New England west to southern Ontario, west central Wisconsin and southern Minnesota, south through eastern Kansas, eastern Oklahoma and central Texas, east to central Georgia, and north along the Atlantic coast.

Ecology: Pine voles are found in a wide range of habitats, from sea level to over 2,500 feet. They prefer woodlands and grasslands, but have been found in rocky areas, marshes and swamps.

Their burrows are extensive and most often are dug 3 to 4 inches below the surface. Sometimes they will cache up to a gallon of fruits, tubers and roots. They make round nests of shredded plant stems, leaves and roots. The nest is 6 to 7 inches in diameter, is usually found under rocks, logs, stumps or debris, and has three or four exits. These nests harbor great numbers of insects.

Man, short-tailed shrews, house cats, skunks, weasels, dogs, foxes, coyotes, raccoons, mink, owls, hawks, and snakes prey on pine voles. They have mites, lice, fleas and internal parasites.

Behavior: Pine voles are active all year and while they seldom emerge from a burrow, they might do so at night. They are gregarious and aggressive and often fight among themselves. They chatter harshly when fighting and have a double or single alarm note.

Pine voles can run up to 3.8 miles an hour; they are poor climbers but good swimmers. They do not range far and have home territories in the 30-yard range.

They eat a wide variety of bulbs, tubers, seeds, berries, acorns, bark, leaves, and roots. Sometimes they eat animal matter.

The breeding season is from mid-February to mid-November. The young are born about 24 days after mating. Litters have two to four young. They are born blind, naked and helpless. They are weaned by the 17th day and become sexually mature at 2 months.

Muskrat
Ondatra zibethicus

About the size of a house cat, the muskrat gets its name from a pair of prominent glands located near the anus. These glands give off a musky odor which is particularly strong in breeding season.

Description: The muskrat has a long, thick tail which is higher than it is wide, sparsely haired, and covered with small scales. It serves as a rudder and scull for swimming.

The head is broad and blunt with small, beady black eyes and short hair-covered ears that barely extend beyond the fur. The small forefeet have four sharp claws and a thumbnail for digging. The hind feet are large and broad with five clawed toes that are partly webbed and fringed with short, stiff hairs.

The coat has dense, soft, almost waterproof gray underfur with long, brown, glossy guard hairs. Males and females look alike. The back is rich brown, darkest on the head and nose. The sides are grayish brown to russet. The underparts vary from pale gray to bright cinnamon. The tail is blackish brown. Dark brown and nearly all black muskrats are not uncommon, and fawn-colored, yellow, silver and albino muskrats occur.

Adults are from 21.7 to 25.3 inches long, with a tail 9.9 to 12.6 inches and a hind foot 3.2 to 3.6 inches. They weigh from 1.5 to 4 pounds.

Distribution: Muskrats are found over most of North America north of Mexico, except for Florida, a coastal strip in Georgia and South Carolina, and most of Texas and California.

Ecology: Swamps, bogs, creeks, canals, ponds, lakes, slow-moving streams and drainage ditches are all home to the semi-aquatic muskrat. It may dig a den in a bank or build one of water plants. A bank den may have one or more chambers well above water. One or more underwater entrances open into tunnels that slope up to the chamber, which contains a bulky nest of dried vegetation.

When banks aren't available, a house is built in about 2 feet of water; it is typically shaped like a cone and made of piled-up cattails roots and stalks, plant remains, and mud brought from the surrounding bottom. A tunnel is gnawed from the bottom upward through the foundation. More vegetation and mud are then heaped on top. As the roof settles, the builders gnaw away at the ceiling until there is an inner chamber a foot or more in diameter. Usually the chamber is a few inches above water level and is lined with clean, fine grasses. The walls are at least a foot thick. Each house usually has two or more underwater entrances. Houses may be 1 to 4 feet high and 8 to 10 feet in diameter at water level.

Muskrats continue building throughout the year. They also build feeding or shelter huts surrounding the main house; they can bring food into these smaller versions of their main houses to eat without interference from predators or weather.

As soon as ice forms in winter, muskrats will often cut a 4 to 5-inch hole in it and push up a fine pile of bottom plants until a

MUSKRAT

pile 12 to 18 inches high is made. In this pile the muskrat will construct a cavity at ice level which serves as a shelter and breathing space and may be used as a feeding station. These "breather houses" collapse when the ice melts.

Man, mink, dogs, coyotes, red foxes, raccoons, skunks, otters, weasels, bobcats, house cats, great horned owls, marsh hawks, snapping turtles, large snakes, pickerel, bass, and northern pike prey on muskrats. They have fleas and internal parasites and are subject to several diseases.

Behavior: Active throughout the year, muskrats are mainly night animals. They are wary and aggressive and may attack if approached too closely.

Muskrats tend to be territorial, particularly females with young. For most of the year they live singly or with mates, but several may share a winter house. Their normal range is within 200 yards of their home or den.

They move mainly in spring and fall, and may move overland more than 20 miles in search of better habitat. High water at the advent of breeding season will force them to move as will drought.

Muskrats spend much of their lives in tunnels, burrows and houses, or in the water. They cannot endure severe cold or freezing wind; abrupt weather changes can kill them.

Muskrats are quiet except during mating, when the female makes loud, birdlike squeals. They swim and dive like a beaver at 1 to 3 miles an hour. They can stay underwater for 15 minutes or more. Sometimes they make a warning splash with their tails.

Muskrats mainly eat aquatic plants, but will consume almost any succulent, tender growth, including corn, alfalfa, soybeans, carrots, and apples. They eat insects, freshwater clams, crayfish, snails, mussels, frogs, reptiles, turtles, minnows, sluggish fish, young birds, and carrion.

In the north, muskrats probably first breed in March, the first litter being born in April or May, a second in June or July, and possibly a third in August. Birth occurs 28 or 30 days after mating with one to fourteen in the litter, the average being six or seven. Newborns are blind, helpless and almost naked. The young are noisy, and squeal when disturbed. Their eyes open by 16 days, and they are weaned at about 2 months. They live 3 to 4 years.

Southern Bog Lemming
Synaptomys cooperi

Sphagnum moss bogs are the primary home of the southern bog lemming, but these creatures are sometimes found in woodlands.

Description: They resemble eastern meadow voles, but are smaller, with a much shorter tail. The eyes are small and the ears nearly concealed in long, shaggy hair. The lips close behind orange incisor teeth when they gnaw. The tail is scarcely longer than the hind foot. The front foot has four toes and the hind foot five.

Males and females look alike. The back is brown to chestnut, with a grizzled look. The sides and underparts are silvery. The tail is brownish above and whitish below. The feet are brownish black. Old males may have white hairs growing from the center of hip glands. Albino and black southern bog lemmings are rare.

Adults are 4.5 to 5.3 inches long with a tail .7 to .9 inch. They weigh from .7 to 1.4 ounces.

Distribution: Southern bog lemmings are found from Godbout, Quebec, west to southeastern Manitoba, south to southwestern Kansas, east through northern Arkansas and Kentucky, south to western North Carolina and Virginia and western Maryland to the Atlantic coastal plain of Maryland, Delaware and New Jersey, and northward through New England to Cape Breton Island.

Ecology: They prefer to live in deep, thick leaf mold where their burrows form complex tunnels. The burrows are 1 to 2 inches in diameter, and there are side tunnels for food storage, feeding and resting. The burrows are up to a foot below ground. They also have well-defined surface runways which may contain little piles of cut grass.

The nest is usually in an enlarged section of the burrow and is lined with dried grasses and sedges. The nest is 6 to 8 inches in diameter and has two to four entrances.

Man, most predatory mammals, hawks, owls, and snakes prey on them. They have fleas, lice and internal parasites.

Behavior: Southern bog lemmings live in small colonies and are often found with other small rodents. They are active all year and are mostly night animals.

Southern bog lemmings are gentle and travel slowly, although they move fast when frightened. They swim well, and have a home range of about 1 square acre.

Their food is succulent leaves, stems and seeds of grasses and sedges, and sometimes fungi, moss, ground pine, bark and insects.

They breed year round, with birth 21 to 23 days after mating. They have several litters a year, with one to eight young. The newborn are blind, naked and helpless. The eyes open on the 12th day.

Northern Bog Lemming
Synaptomys borealis shagnicola

The northern bog lemming looks much like the southern bog lemming. Probably the best distinguishing characteristic is that the female northern has eight nipples, compared to six for the southern.

Description: Males and females look alike—dull brown on the back, brighter on the rump. The underparts are grayish and the tail brownish above and paler below. The feet are dark grayish to almost black.

Males and females are the same size, 4.6 to 5.3 inches long, with a tail .7 to 1.1 inches long. They weigh 1.1 to 1.2 ounces.

Distribution: They are found from Alaska and British Columbia south to northern Washington and Idaho, across Canada to northern Wisconsin, and northward to Labrador.

Ecology: Northern bog lemmings are found in cold sphagnum bogs, bluegrass fields matted with weeds, and dense hemlock and beech woods.

They may make crisscrossing runways or may burrow just beneath leaf mold. The nest is lined with dried leaves and grasses and sometimes fur. The nest may be several inches underground or just beneath the surface. Its enemies are probably the same as those that prey on the southern bog lemming.

Behavior: Little is known about the life of the northern bog lemming. These creatures may be found living in colonies or dwelling in the burrows of other small mammals. They are known to eat raspberry seeds. In reproduction, they probably are like the southern bog lemming.

NORTHERN BOG LEMMING

Old World Rats and Mice

This family, known as Muridae, has been introduced into North America from Europe. Its members all have three cheek teeth, both above and below, on each side of the jaw. Through introduction by man, these rodents are nearly cosmopolitan.

Norway Rat

Rattus norvegicus

Norway rats eat almost anything and will consume one-third of their body weight in 24 hours. They are pests throughout the world. Beyond being repulsive, they are a health menace and an economic burden. Rats and their parasites have caused worldwide epidemics, the most terrible being bubonic plague or "black death," which killed 25 million Europeans in the 14th Century and 10 million people in India from 1898 to 1923.

Description: The Norway rat has ears partly hidden in its fur and a scaly, nearly hairless tail that is shorter than the length of the head and body. The front foot has four clawed toes and a small clawless thumb. The hind foot has five clawed toes.

The fur is coarse, and males and females are the same color, reddish brown to grayish brown on the back and sides, mixed with scattered black hairs. The underparts are silvery or yellowish white. The tail is dark gray above, lighter below. The feet are grayish or dull white above. Color phases include whites, blacks, pieds or blotched gray-blacks, and the commercial albino laboratory rat.

Males are somewhat larger than females. Adults are 12 to 18 inches long, with a tail 5.9 to 8.8 inches and a hind foot 1.6 to 1.8 inches. They weigh up to 1.5 pounds.

Distribution: Apparently originating in Asia, the Norway rat arrived in North America on the Atlantic seaboard about 1775. It occurs throughout North America.

Ecology: Extremely adaptable, Norway rats are found wherever there is food, water and shelter for them. They are found in,

under, and adjacent to buildings and dumps, along streams and rivers, in marshy areas and sewers, on waterfronts, and occasionally in open fields.

Excellent diggers, Norway rats make extensive burrows 2 to 3 inches in diameter, normally 12 inches deep, and about 36 inches long. Each burrow has one or more emergency exits well hidden under boards or grass. The den is 4 to 6 inches in diameter and is used as a refuge, breeding nest and place to eat. It is lined with paper, cloth, vegetation or any other shreddable material.

Man, large hawks and owls, foxes, dogs, house cats, mink, skunks, weasels and snakes prey on them. Perhaps their chief enemies are the diseases salmonellosis, tularemia, leptospiral jaundice, Haverhill fever and murine typhus fever. They have fleas, mites, ticks and internal parasites.

Behavior: Active throughout the year, Norway rats are mostly nocturnal. They are sensitive to light but don't see well. Their sense of smell, taste, touch and hearing are highly developed. Norway rats continually sniff, and they leave scent trails which are followed by other rats.

The ability of Norway rats to detect even minute amounts of poison is what leads to their "bait shyness." They can hear sounds in the ultrasonic range, 20 to 40 thousand cycles per second.

Inquisitive and constantly exploring, they quickly detect new objects and avoid them, preferring established, protected routes. Excellent swimmers, they are fairly good climbers. They like water and have been reported to dive 80 feet.

They are gregarious and social, and form colonies composed of several families, sharing nesting and feeding areas. They will fight other rats that invade their territory.

Dominant males take the most favorable places near food supplies and defend burrow systems containing several females.

Cold weather will sometimes force them to move from the outside into buildings, but normally they remain in deep burrows in dumps year round. Some wander extensively. If food and water are far apart, they will travel frequently.

They thrive on meats and fish, vegetables, grains, fruits, nuts, garden crops, eggs and roots. Garbage offers them a balanced diet. They are known to kill poultry, wild birds, young pigs and lambs, black rats, rattlesnakes, fingerling fish, and even their own young in unguarded nests. They will gnaw through lead pipes to get to water and have been known to gnaw leather, cloth, soap, paint, books and all sorts of packaged goods. They need about 1½ ounces of water per day.

Norway rats are polygamous and breed throughout the year, peaking in spring and autumn. The young are born about 21 to 22 days after mating, and a female will have three to twelve litters a year. The number of young varies from six to twenty-two. The newborn are naked, blind, pink and helpless. They are weaned at about 3 weeks and reach sexual maturity between 80 and 85 days. They live about 3 years.

House Mouse
Mus musculus

The house mouse has probably been in North America as long as the white man, no doubt arriving hidden among the possessions of the first colonists.

Description: A small gray mouse with a long, pointed nose, the house mouse has a long tail with scanty fine hairs and scales tinged yellowish gray. Males and females look alike. Some are piebald, leaden or other shades of gray, all white or black. Commercial white mice are a mutation of the house mouse. Adults are 6.2 to 7.8 inches long, with a tail 2.7 to 3.7 inches long. They weigh .53 to 1.05 ounces.

Distribution: They are found along the coast of Alaska, from southern Canada throughout the United States, and through Mexico to Panama.

Ecology: House mice are most often found in or near human habitations and in fields, hay shocks, wheat ricks, and corncribs. The nest may be made of shredded paper, cloth or grass. Sometimes they build communal nests.

Man, birds of prey, foxes, coyotes, house cats, shrews, weasels, meadow voles, skunks, rats, and snakes prey on them. They have many parasites and transmit human bacterial and viral diseases. They are known to carry murine typhus fever, leptospirosis and salmonellosis. They get mange.

House mice are known to "waltz" by twisting around on one foot, this is apparently the result of inbreeding. Some mice are "shakers"—they make nervous head movements, circle, and are deaf.

Behavior: Active year round, house mice are mainly night animals. Some move indoors in winter and back out in spring.

In a house they scurry about and gnaw woodwork, dropping little black scats wherever they go. In the wild they form loose colonies in which the males are aggressive and fight.

Nervous and curious, house mice usually walk slowly, stopping often to sniff and poke around. They can run up to 8 miles an hour. They are great climbers and jumpers and swim well. Normally quiet, they squeak when trapped or hurt.

Occasionally a house mouse will sing. No one knows why. The song sounds like a cricket but is much more continuous. The

HOUSE MOUSE

senses of smell, taste, vision, touch and hearing are all well developed. The long whiskers and guard hairs are sensitive to touch. While house mice frequently groom themselves, they commonly foul their environment.

House mice will eat almost any kind of food but favor sweet and high protein items. They feed 15 to 20 times a day and take in about 10% of their body weight each day. They are known to eat glue, paste, and soap, and gnaw household items such as paper, books, leather, wood, cardboard, lead, most plastics, and clothing. They cache food at times.

Prolific breeders, they have up to eight litters a year, with 3 to 8 young in each. Peak breeding times are spring and late summer. The young are born 19 to 21 days after breeding and are naked, pink, blind and helpless. They are weaned at 3 weeks and females are sexually mature at 8 weeks. They live to two years in the wild and up to 6 years in captivity.

Jumping Mice

These small to medium-sized mouselike rodents are in the family Zapodidae. They have long tails and large hind feet made for jumping. Jumping mice are found in Eurasia and North America from the southern arctic area of Canada south to about 35 degrees north latitude.

Meadow Jumping Mouse
Zapus hudsonius

Of the hibernating mammals, the meadow jumping mouse is among the deepest of sleepers. It also hibernates as long or longer than the others, going into hibernation as early as mid-September and emerging as late as early May.

Description: These mice have greatly elongated hind legs and a tapering, slender, scaly tail longer than the head and body. The small eyes are located midway between the nose and ears. The ears are large, scantily haired and partially hidden in the fur, which is long and coarse.

Males and females look alike. The guard hairs are black or brown. The underfur is grayish or whitish near the skin and yellowish brown on top. In summer the upper parts are yellowish olive or yellowish brown mixed with the black-tipped guard hairs, forming a back band from head to tail. The underparts are white, sometimes washed with yellow. The tail is grayish brown above and yellowish white below, with a tuft of black hairs on the end. The ears are edged with white or buff. White-spotted meadow jumping mice have been reported.

Females are slightly larger than males. Adults are 7.3 to 9.9 inches long, with a tail 4.2 to 6 inches long. They weigh .5 to .8 ounce.

Distribution: They are found from Alaska and northern Canada south into Colorado, eastern Alabama, northern Georgia, and South Carolina.

Ecology: The meadow jumping mouse is commonly found in moist, grassy fields, in brush and along streams, ponds and marshes with rank vegetation.

The nest might be found on a grass hummock, under logs or planks, in hollow logs, or at least 6 inches underground.

The nest is made of grass, leaves or other soft vegetation, and is 6 inches in diameter, with a small entrance hole near the top. The hibernating nest is 3 or more inches underground or in a gravel pit, sand bank, woodchuck den, potato hill, small mammal burrow, or in clumps of bayberry bushes.

Man, coyotes, foxes, mink, house cats, red-tailed hawks, barn

MEADOW JUMPING MOUSE

owls, long-eared owls, snakes, northern pike and bass prey on them. They have fleas, ticks, mites and internal parasites.

Behavior: Essentially solitary, meadow jumping mice are active mostly at night. They hibernate singly or in pairs rolled into a ball.

The name jumping mouse is misleading. Mostly, they travel slowly through the grass or take little hops of up to six inches. They are good swimmers and can dive. They climb over brush and grass stems. They often wash their faces, feet and tails. The adults are usually silent but make a clucking sound and a series of chirps and also drumming noises by vibrating their tails. They can dig in loose soil, and will use the burrows of other animals.

They eat grass seeds, fruits of shrubs, berries, nuts, tomatoes, melons, sunflower seeds, roots, fungi, earthworms, spiders, insects and slugs.

The breeding season extends from May to October, peaking in the first three weeks of June, the first three weeks of August and sometimes the first two weeks of September. Most females have two litters a year with two to eight young. They are born naked, blind and helpless. They are fully furred by the 17th day. They live to nearly 2 years.

Woodland Jumping Mouse

Napaeozapus insignis

Woodland jumping mice can leap up to 6 feet. They travel on all four feet when moving slowly and take hops for greater speed.

Description: The woodland jumping mouse has a white-tipped tail, and has larger ears and more brownish yellow fur than the meadow species. Males and females look alike. They are bright yellow to orange on the flanks and about the face. A broad, brownish black stripe runs the length of the back. The underparts are white. The tail is grayish brown on top and white below.

Females are slightly larger than the males. Adults are 8 to 10.1 inches long with a tail 4.5 to 6.2 inches long. They weigh .5 to 1 ounce.

Distribution: They are found from Cape Breton Island, Prince Edward Island, Nova Scotia, Quebec, south to northern New Jersey, eastern West Virginia and western Maryland, and north to northeastern Ohio.

Ecology: They live in moist, cool woodlands along banks of mountain streams. They make shallow runways but mostly use burrows made by moles, shrews and other small mammals. Nests may be in brush piles, under stumps or rotting logs, or several inches underground. The nest is made of dry grass and

WOODLAND JUMPING MOUSE

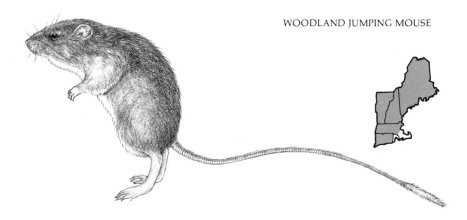

leaves, and is 5 or 6 inches in outside diameter.

Man, house cats, foxes, weasels, skunks, hawks, and owls prey on them. They have mites, fleas and internal parasites.

Behavior: Mainly night animals, they are also active in late morning and early evening hours and on cloudy days. They are deep hibernators.

Woodland jumping mice are elusive, quiet, gentle, and tolerant of their own kind. They are easily tamed. They will give a soft squeal or clucking sound if disturbed while asleep. They have a home range of 1 to 6.5 acres.

They feed on blueberries, huckleberries, raspberries, strawberries, buttercups, mayapples, miterwort, wintergreen, small seeds and nuts, leaves, spleenwort, roots, fungi, insects, moths, caterpillars, beetles, larvae, grubs, earthworms and millipedes.

They breed from late May to late August, with one or two litters a year. The young are born 21 to 25 days after mating in litters of one to eight. Newborns are naked, blind and helpless. They are weaned at 22 to 25 days, and become sexually mature at about six weeks.

American Porcupines

Porcupines are large, robust rodents with long, sharp quills that can be raised or lowered. They are slow, clumsy and deliberate, both on land and in trees. The legs are short and the soles of the hind feet are heavy and calloused. They conduct complex courtship before mating.

Porcupine
Erethizon dorsatum dorsatum

The story persists, but the porcupine cannot throw any of the 30,000 or so quills on its body. It can flip its tail, and some of the loose quills may fall out, since they are often loosely attached to the skin.

Description: The head is small, with a rounded, blunt muzzle, hairy lips, small ears and dull black eyes. The legs are short and bowed. The front foot has four toes and the hind foot five, all with sharp claws. The tail is short and heavy.

Porcupines have three kinds of hairs. There is a long, soft, woolly underfur overlaid with long, stiff, glistening guard hairs, mixed with the still longer quills. The quills are 3 to 4 inches long and hollow. The tips are needlelike and covered with hundreds of tiny backward-slanting, diamond-shaped scales that act as barbs. The quills are found all over the upper body, from the crown of the head to the end of the tail. The feet and underparts of the body and tail are quill-less.

When cornered, a porcupine erects its quills, tucks its head between its front feet, and turns its rear to its opponent while rapidly swinging its tail or making rolling lunges of the body. Once a quill is embedded it absorbs moisture and expands. The quills tend to work their way in deeper, with time.

A quill or fragment may travel at an inch a day in flesh, causing intense pain, and eventually reach a vital organ, causing death.

Males and females are alike in coloring. In summer they are glossy black or brownish black all over, with or without white-tipped guard hairs. The bases of the quills are yellowish white and the tips are brown or black. The winter coat is darker, duller and longer.

Males are heavier than females. They are 25 to 40 inches long, with a tail 5.7 to 11.7 inches and a hind foot 2.9 to 3.5 inches. They weigh 5 to 25 pounds.

Distribution: Porcupines are found from Nova Scotia, Quebec, and Alaska across Canada, south through the northeastern states, south along the Appalachian Mountains of western Maryland, in West Virginia, west through Indiana and Iowa, south through northwestern Texas and northern Mexico, and northward through the Pacific states. They are found in all the New England states but are uncommon in Rhode Island.

Ecology: They live in mixed hardwood-evergreen woodlands where they can find den sites. Porcupines prefer hemlock and sugar maple areas and are found in valleys as well as on mountaintops. The den may be in a cave, a deep rock crevice, a hollow log, a deserted fox den, a beaver burrow, or under a stump or abandoned building.

Man and fishers are the porcupine's chief predators, but these creatures are also killed by lynx, bobcats, coyotes, gray foxes, dogs and owls. They suffer from lice, ticks, internal parasites, mange, and a disease called "snuffles" in which a green mucous flows from the nose.

Behavior: Active all year, porcupines are mostly night animals and spend the day perched high in a tree or hidden in a den. They rely greatly on hearing and smell. They are nearsighted, and this leads to much of their "stupid" actions.

They are sure-footed and persistent, though slow and waddling. They can gallop at about 2 miles an hour. They climb easily, arm over arm, but descend clumsily backwards. They do not like water but can swim.

PORCUPINE

Gnawing Mammals   109

Porcupines make a wide variety of sounds including moans, shrieks, owl-like hoots, shrill screeches, barks, whines, grunts, coughs, sniffs, chatters, snorts, mews, and sobs—like a child crying.

Mostly solitary, porcupines will den in small groups in winter. The dens serve as protection from wind, snow and predators. Dens aren't protected, and many different porcupines may use one on a rotating basis. A den can usually be recognized by large piles of droppings. Some porcupines will spend the winter in a "station tree," usually a hemlock or white spruce. They may defend winter feeding trees. In summer they often climb trees to avoid mosquitoes.

Most of a porcupine's time is spent in a tree; these animals are not great travelers. They eat a variety of grasses and sedges, leaves, pond lilies, apples, sweet corn, farm crops, twigs, forbs, roots, buds, flowers, catkins, and sugar maple seeds, and the bark of hemlock, white cedar, larch, balsam, white pine, basswood, beech, American elm, American chestnut, gray birch, paper birch, yellow birch, large tooth aspen, quaking aspen, pin cherry, poplar, red maple, red oak, white ash, and other hardwoods.

Porcupines love salt and will gnaw on anything to get it, including axe handles, oars and paddles. They also like to chew on shed deer antlers.

The breeding season begins in early November and lasts through December. Some females may breed in late March or April. The courtship is elaborate, with much noise. The male will do a three-legged walk, usually with his left forepaw holding his genitals. He may hold a stick in his front feet, straddling and riding it. The male usually urinates on the female.

Despite popular fiction, porcupines do not mate while standing belly to belly; they copulate with the usual rear mount. After mating, the female ejects a bluish white vaginal plug about a half-inch long. Usually a single young is born, called "Porcupette." The female usually takes little or no care of the young, born from April to June, after the first week or two. The newborn are able to move about, and are covered with long black hair and quills that soon become functional. When six months old, the young porcupine will drift away from its mother. Porcupines are sexually mature at 15 to 16 months, and they live to 10 years in the wild.

6. Whales, Dolphins and Porpoises

THE LARGEST ANIMALS IN THE WORLD belong to the order called Cetaceans. Some live in rivers, some enter large inland lakes, but most inhabit the oceans and seas.

They can be identified by bodies tapered at both ends, forelimbs modified into flippers, laterally flattened tails (the fins of which are called "flukes"), and the lack of external hind legs. The dorsal, or back, fin has no bones. The skin is thick, smooth, and nearly hairless. The body has a thick layer of insulating blubber.

These animals have a "melon"—a lens-shaped fatty deposit in the facial depression of the skull which apparently serves as an echolocation lens.

There are 2 suborders of Cetaceans which are greatly different in anatomy. They are the Odontoceti, or toothed whales, dolphins, and porpoises, and the Mysticeti, or baleen or whalebone whales.

Toothed Whales

The toothed whales (suborder Odontoceti) have a single blow-hole, a relatively small mouth, and from few to many teeth. They catch relatively large prey one at a time and usually feed on fish and squid.

Beaked Whales

These medium-sized whales in the Ziphiidae family have well-developed beaks that merge sharply into a bulging forehead in some species and gradually in others. They have two conspicuous grooves on the throat forming a V shape and a sickle-shaped dorsal fin located well behind the middle of the body. Their flippers are small and set close together, and their flukes are not usually separated by a notch. The adults have only one or two pairs of teeth, only in the lower jaw. Females have reduced teeth that sometimes do not erupt above the gums. Not much is known of their behavior.

North Atlantic Beaked Whale
Mesoplodon bidens

The only known instance of this whale off New England shores was in 1867, when one was stranded on Nantucket Island, Massachusetts.

Description: The head is somewhat flattened and the forehead is moderately high, gradually tapering to a long, slender beak. In adults the lower jaw protrudes somewhat. The lower jaw has a relatively large pair of teeth, and some small teeth may also be present.

Color varies from black or bluish black to dark gray above and grayish to whitish below. Some have many white scars or scratches over the body. The flukes may be dusky or whitish.

These whales may be 14.8 to 18 feet long.

Distribution: They are found only in the North Atlantic Ocean

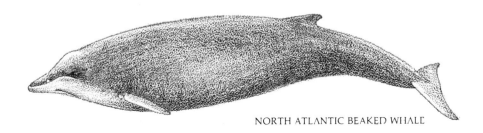

NORTH ATLANTIC BEAKED WHALE

and adjacent seas, and are well known from European coasts.

Behavior: This species has been found singly and in pairs in the North Atlantic in all seasons. It may feed on cephlapods and deep sea fishes. The breeding season may be in the fall.

Tropical Beaked Whale
Mesoplodon densirostris

The only record of this whale in New England waters was a female taken at Annisquam, Massachusetts, in 1898.

Description: This whale is distinguished by an enormous lower jaw bearing a pair of large, triangular, tusklike teeth found only in males. They are nearly all black, with slightly paler bellies.
    Measurements of three whales ranged from 14.4 to 14.8 feet with the largest weighing 1,784 pounds.

Distribution: A warm-water species, this whale appears widely distributed in tropical and sub-tropical waters. Sick or injured individuals may drift to colder waters.

Behavior: This species is little known.

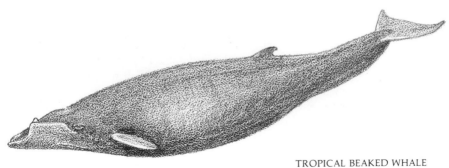

TROPICAL BEAKED WHALE

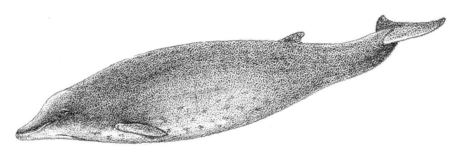

TRUE'S BEAKED WHALE

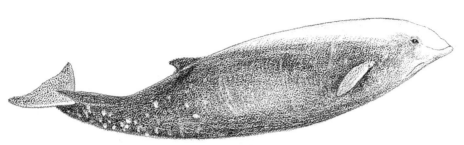

GOOSE-BEAKED WHALE

True's Beaked Whale

Mesoplodon mirus

Description: Generally similar to other whales in this family, the True's beaked whale has a pair of small teeth in the lower jaw, located at the tip. (On females, these are concealed in the gums.)

In dead specimens, the color of the upper parts is slate black, fading to slate gray on the sides and underparts. The lower sides and underparts may have small, long spots of light purple, yellow or pink. Sometimes there is a dark line in the center of the belly. There may be a dark gray area on the thorax.

Measurements of 5 females ranged from 16.1 to 17.1 feet, and a male was 14.4 feet. The estimated weight of the largest female was between 2,500 and 3,000 pounds.

Distribution: They are found principally in the northwestern Atlantic.

Behavior: The species is little known. The stomachs of beached specimens have contained squid and fish.

Goose-beaked Whale

Ziphius cavirostris

The shape of the forehead and snout give this whale its name.

Description: The beak is short and rounded and looks triangular from above. The lower jaw extends beyond the upper. The back fin is located about two-thirds down the length of the body. There is a single pair of teeth at the tip of the lower jaw, and in females these are usually concealed in the gums.

These whales are dark brown or grayish black, frequently pale white around the face and as far back as the dorsal fin. Adults often have lots of blotches, mostly on the flanks. Some have whitish scars or scratches.

This whale may reach a length of 30 feet. The weight of a 19-foot male was 5,590 pounds.

Distribution: The goose-beaked whale inhabits most oceans but does not seem to be common in any. Occasional strandings have been reported along the New England coast.

Behavior: They have been reported to travel in groups of 30 to 40 and feed together, while other reports say they are usually solitary. Goose-beaked whales are reported to stay submerged for more than 30 minutes. Squid appears to be their favored food. Most births seem to occur in autumn. At birth the calf is about one-third the length of the female.

Bottle-nosed Whale
Hyperoodon ampullatus

Large bottle-nosed whales, especially males, have a high forehead that descends to a short beak at almost a right angle, giving the animal the appearance which results in its name.

Description: The body is thickest between the back fin and flippers. The mouth is cleft and slightly S-shaped laterally. They have 1 or 2 pairs of teeth in the tip of the lower jaw; these are very small in females.

Color varies with age. Young whales are brownish and often spotted with yellowish white on the flanks and belly. Adults are dark gray above and lighter below. Some adult males have cream-colored heads. The flippers and flukes are darker than the body. Old bottle-nosed whales may be all cream-colored.

Males are larger than females. They are 25 to 30 feet long, while females are 20 to 23 feet long.

Distribution: The bottle-nosed whale occurs in all oceans of the northern hemisphere. It is found in the North Atlantic in summer, and sometimes migrates to the Mediterranean in winter.

Behavior: Observers have reported that these whales travel in small schools of 20 or more and that they remain underwater up to 20 minutes when feeding, probably on squid and fish. The gestation period is about 12 months, and calves are born in spring and summer.

BOTTLE-NOSED WHALE

Sperm Whales

This family gets its name from the spermaceti organ located in the head. The name spermaceti is derived from the Latin words sperma ceti, meaning "whale sperm," based on the erroneous belief that the substance was coagulated semen.

In sperm whales the lower jaw is much narrower than the contour of the head. These mammals occur in all oceans.

Sperm Whale

Physeter catodon

Sperm whales are the source of ambergris, an abnormal waxy material that comes from the digestive tract. It is often expelled by the whales and may be found floating or washed ashore.

Ambergris was used as medicine by ancient civilizations and today as a fragrance fixing material for perfume. The color varies from blackish or yellowish brown to whitish. Fresh ambergris

SPERM WHALE

has a disagreeable smell, but after exposure it hardens and gives off a sweet odor. The largest recorded lump weighed 1,003 pounds. It brings $10 to $50 a pound, depending on color. It was reported that $60,000 worth was removed from the intestines of one whale.

Sperm whales have been slaughtered indiscriminately in the past. They are now protected in United States waters.

Description: The largest of the toothed whales, it has a barrel-shaped head and narrow, log-like lower jaw with rows of teeth. The head is high, thick and blunt. The blow hole is located on the left front end of the head. The spout is directed to the left and forward at a 45-degree angle. The small eyes are just above and behind the angle of the mouth.

The back fin is low and thick, compressed into a hump, followed by additional humps. The skin is bumpy on the back and flanks. The flippers are small and located a little below and behind the eyes. The flukes are large, triangular, and separated by a deep notch.

Sperm whales are usually brown, sometimes slate gray, except for occasional patches of white on the lower jaw and belly. Adult males are sometimes pale or piebald. All-white sperm whales have been taken in the Pacific.

Adult males are larger than females and may reach 60 feet long and weigh 50 tons.

Distribution: Sperm whales are found in all oceans and prefer deep oceans. They are rare in New England waters.

Behavior: Sperm whales are social and may form groups of 1,000 or more. They can leap completely out of the water. They lobtail by getting perpendicular in the water and slapping the water with their flukes. This may be used as a signal to gather. They can hear the distress calls of other whales at distances of up to 7 miles. These whales make low-pitched groans, muffled swashing noises and a series of sharp clicks. At times they will raise their heads in the air and look completely around. Normally timid, when provoked or injured they may be dangerous. Sometimes large males fight.

Sperm whales are deep divers, descending to over 3,000 feet. The larger the whale, the longer and deeper it will dive. They have been known to dive for more than an hour, and when they surface they blow approximately once for each minute underwater.

When they emerge, the top of the head comes out first. When the blowhole clears the water, a spout is blown 10 to 12 feet high. The sound can be heard from more than 800 feet.

They normally swim at 2 to 4 knots. When frightened they may hit 12 knots, and harpooned sperm whales have pulled whaleboats from 10 to 21 knots.

They feed deep in the ocean on large squid, octopuses, sharks, skates and other fish. Squid up to 34.5 feet long and weighing 578 pounds have been found in the stomach of a sperm whale.

Sperm whales are polygamous, and males form harems in the breeding season; this lasts from January to July in the north. Gestation takes 16 to 17 months. At birth the calves are about 12.5 feet long and will nurse for about a year. The female is strongly attached to her young and will remain near her wounded young until it dies or recovers. Females become sexually mature at about 9 years and males at 9½. They may live up to 50 years.

Pygmy Sperm Whale
Kogia breviceps

As the name implies, this is a miniature version of its large relative.

Description: The pygmy sperm whale has a sharklike mouth with functional teeth only in the lower jaw, a porpoiselike shape, and exaggerated head proportions. The blowhole is located above the eyes, and the back fin is well formed.

These whales are dark gray above and light gray below. The lower jaw may be whitish.

Males are larger than females. They are 6.6 to 13.1 feet long and weigh 700 to 920 pounds.

Distribution: Pygmy sperm whales are widely distributed in the temperate and tropical oceans of the world.

Behavior: Not much is known about their activities, but they might migrate toward the poles in summer and return to warmer waters in winter. They feed on crabs, squid, shrimp and fish.

Breeding probably occurs in late summer, and the calves may be born the following spring. Females produce a single calf which is weaned at one year. They are probably sexually mature at 2 years.

White Whales and Narwhales

There are only 2 members in this family of whales known as Monodontidae. The narwhale is not known in New England waters. The male has a straight, twisted tusk which may get to almost 10 feet long, that grows from the left upper tooth.

In both narwhales and white whales the dorsal fin is absent or tiny, the flippers short, broad and rounded.

White Whale
Delphinapterus leucas

Easily identified by their all-white coloration, white whales have the odd habit of swallowing mud, sand and stones while feeding at the bottom.

Description: The white whale has a high, rounded forehead and a short, broad snout, no back fin, and teeth on both upper and lower jaws.

At birth they are dark brown, then turn gray and finally lighten to white or ivory.

Males are larger than females. They range from 496 to 1,488 pounds. Males reach 17 feet long and females 15 feet.

WHITE WHALE

Distribution: White whales, also called belugas, and found throughout arctic and subarctic seas. In severe winter weather they may straggle as far south as New Jersey.

Behavior: White whales usually travel in small family groups but have been found in gatherings of up to 10,000 animals. They migrate as far north as ice permits. All-male schools of up to 1,000 have been recorded.

They have well developed hearing and sight. They can chirp, click, growl, squeal and creak, and often emit low grunting sounds like a pig and trilling noises like a songbird.

Normal swimming speeds are 3 to 4 knots, and when scared they will hit 8 knots. Normally they dive for 2 minutes but can stay under for 15 minutes. They use their backs to break thin ice and keep air holes open. They are able to scull with their tails to swim backwards.

Capelin are the primary food of the white whale, but these animals also eat sand launce, cod, tomcod, sculpins, paddleworms and squid.

White whales are polygamous and breed in the spring. The calves are born 14 months after conception and nurse for about 20 months. At birth they are 4 to 6 feet long. They live about 25 years.

Dolphins and Porpoises

The delphinids are swift swimmers, and many species make synchronized leaps clear of the water. They are known for riding the bow waves of ships.

The name "dolphin" is usually applied to members of this family which have a beaklike snout and slender body. "Porpoise" generally refers to those with blunt snouts and stocky bodies. Both are shallow divers which surface often. They are gregarious. Dolphins will sometimes kill sharks by ramming them.

STRIPED DOLPHIN

Striped Dolphin
Stenella cacruleoalba

The best identification mark of the striped dolphin is the "bilge stripe" which runs from the eye to the anus.

Description: The forehead and back are dark steel blue. The chin, throat and lower half of the flanks and belly are white. A dark blue stripe starts from the back fin and ends abruptly in front. A narrow stripe extends from the eye, which is circled with blue, to the base of the dark blue flipper. The dorsal fin and flukes are dark blue, but the bottom of the flukes is white.

Males are bigger than females. Adults are 7.9 to 8.9 feet long.

Distribution: They are found in the warmer waters of the Atlantic Ocean and Pacific Ocean but have been reported as far north as Greenland. This species is rare in New England waters.

Behavior: Striped dolphins have been found in schools of up to 3,000 animals. Squid is reported to be their main food.

They breed in spring and fall. Calving may occur in spring or fall, and the young nurse for 6 to 12 months. They become sexually mature at about 4 years old.

Common Dolphin
Delphinus delphis

The common dolphin sometimes ascends rivers but is not a common visitor to New England waters.

Description: The body is dark gray to brownish black above and white below. The blackish coloring, widest at the top of each side of the back fin, forms a marking like a saddle. The sides and flanks are varying shades of yellowish gray marked with long bands of gray, white or yellow. Across the forehead is a whitish band with a narrow black stripe that unites with black eye rings. The flippers are somewhat lighter on the bottom. The flukes are blackish on both sides.

Distribution: The common dolphin is widely distributed in temperate and warm waters and is only occasionally found in northern waters of the Atlantic Ocean.

Behavior: A gregarious species, the common dolphin travels in schools of up to several hundred animals. Sociable and playful; these dolphins are sometimes seen leaping about the bows of ships. They are able to swim to speeds of 22 knots but usually swim at less than 5. They feed on squid, octopus and fish.
    They have a long breeding season, from May to November. Gestation lasts 11 months. The newborns are 32 to 37 inches long, and pups are weaned in 4 to 5 months. These dolphins live longer than 20 years.

COMMON DOLPHIN

Bottle-nosed Dolphin

Tursiops truncatus

Swimming at speeds of up to 20 knots, bottle-nosed dolphins can leap vertically from the water for up to 16 feet and catch fish held as bait.

Description: They have a short, depressed beak, clearly divided from the sloping forehead by a furrow. The lower jaw is slightly longer than the upper. The back fin is high and located midway on the body.

Bottle-nosed dolphins are gray or slate gray above, blending to white or grayish white below. There is a dark stripe from the blowhole to the base of the beak and often one or two dark lines from the eye to the beak.

Males are larger than females. Adults are from 8 to 12 feet long and weigh 330 to 440 pounds.

Distribution: Bottle-nosed dolphins are found in coastal temperate and tropical waters of the world. They frequent bays and inshore waters but not rivers. They are uncommon in New England waters.

Behavior: Bottle-nosed dolphins are friendly, gregarious and remarkably intelligent. They form schools from a few to several dozen members. They like to gambol about the bows of moving

BOTTLE-NOSED DOLPHIN

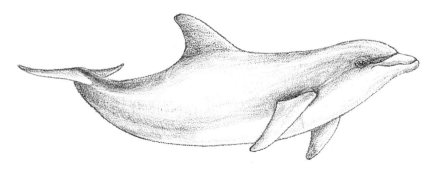

Whales, Dolphins, and Porpoises   125

ships. Females have a strong attachment to their own kind and to other species of dolphins. Adult males seem to dominate the schools.

They are vocal, making pure-tone sounds, whistles and chirps for communication and pulsed sounds or clicks for echolocation.

They feed on mackerel, mullet, cod, kingfish, tarpon, weakfish, roballo, sheepshead, shrimp, squid, rays and other kinds of fish.

Little is known of their reproduction. Most calves are born from March to May after gestation of 11 or 12 months. At birth the calf is over 3 feet long and weighs about 26 pounds. They may nurse for 6 months and achieve sexual maturity at 6 years.

White-beaked Dolphin
Lagenorhynchus albirostris

Description: The white-beaked dolphin is recognized by the white color of the upper beak. The back is dusky, and the flanks sometimes have gray spots. The bottom side is white or creamy. There may be light patches on the flippers, below the back fin, behind the blowhole and near the flukes.

They are from 8.9 to 9.8 feet long.

Distribution: White-beaked dolphins are found in coastal waters of the North Atlantic from the Barents Sea to the coast of France, and from the Davis Strait to Massachusetts.

WHITE-BEAKED DOLPHIN

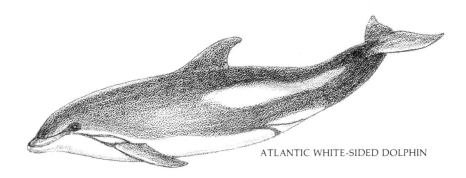

ATLANTIC WHITE-SIDED DOLPHIN

Behavior: They have been found in groups up to 1,500. They eat capelin, mackerel, herring, anchovies, crustaceans, squid and whelks. Calving may occur in summer.

Atlantic White-sided Dolphin
Lagenorhynchus acutus

On September 8, 1974, a group of about 1,000 white-sided dolphins chased a school of herring into Longley Cove near Dennysville, Maine. About 100 animals were stranded by the receding tide, including many pregnant and nursing females. It was the largest group and largest stranding reported for this species.

Description: These dolphins have a relatively small head, with a sloping forehead and very short beak. The back, dorsal fin, flippers and flukes are black. Between the black back and white belly the sides are yellowish gray, except for a wide white band running toward the tail. A streak of yellow or tan runs above the white band up toward, but not over, the ridge of the flukes. A narrow, black stripe runs from the eye to the base of the flipper. There are black circles around the eyes. The lower lip is either white or fringed with black.

Males are larger. Adults measure from 6.6 to 9.8 feet and weigh 340 to 500 pounds.

Distribution: They are common along North Atlantic coasts.

Behavior: White-sided dolphins are commonly found in groups of 1,000 or more. They feed on herring, mackerel, striped bass, salmonids, and some invertebrates.

Calving occurs from spring to midsummer after a 10-month gestation. At birth they are 3.7 to 3.9 feet long.

Killer Whale
Orcinus orca

Killer whales hunt in packs of up to 50 animals and do not hesitate to attack the largest whales. They attack large prey by simultaneously leaping out of the water and tearing flesh with powerful teeth. They often attack penguins and seals that are basking on ice by smashing through with their backs. Sometimes they chase seals up rivers.

KILLER WHALE

Description: The largest member of the dolphin-porpoise family, the killer whale has a prominent back fin. The color is black above and white below. The pattern of white extends upward in two or three lobes on the side of the body. The flippers are black above and below. The flukes are black above, and white fringed with black below. The teeth are cone-shaped, large, and sharp.

Males are much larger than females reaching 30 feet long to only 20 feet for females.

Distribution: Killer whales are cosmopolitan but most common in polar waters. They are rare in New England waters.

Behavior: Killer whales are bold, powerful and ferocious. They swim close together, sometimes in a line. Their black dorsal fins are almost always visible above water.

Their normal swimming speed is 6 knots but they can hit 17 knots without apparent effort. They sound at 1 to 6 minute intervals. They can jump up to 45 feet horizontally and can clear the water by 5 feet. Sometimes they hold their heads out of the water to look around. They have a tightly-knit social order and do not leave their school mates. They make whistles and squeaks for communication and clicks for echolocation.

They feed on squid, fish, sea turtles, sea birds, seals, sea otters, whales, porpoises and dolphins.

The breeding season may last for several months. Pairing occurs in winter. Gestation may take 12 to 16 months and the newborn are about 9 feet long.

Grampus
Grampus griseus

The grampus gets its name from a corruption of the French words *grand poisson,* meaning "big fish."

Description: The grampus has a prominent, rounded forehead that rises almost vertically from the top of the upper jaw. They have only three to seven pairs of teeth in the front of the lower jaw. The dorsal fin is high, pointed and recurved. The flippers are relatively long.

GRAMPUS

COMMON PILOT WHALE

They are grayish black to gray blue or gray tinged with purple above, lighter on the sides and flanks, and paler below. Some have a white, anchor-shaped area between the flippers, extending as far back as the anus. The back fin, flippers and flukes are colored like the back. The forehead is almost white in the young, and the entire head is almost white in old animals.

They range in size from 11.5 to 14.1 feet long.

Distribution: These mammals are widely distributed in temperate and tropical seas. They apparently are rare in New England waters.

Behavior: Grampuses are reported to gather in groups of 60 or more. They appear playful and sometimes leap out of the water and follow ships. They feed on squids and fish.

The young appear to be born between December and March and are 4.6 to 5.6 feet long when born.

Common Pilot Whale
Globicephela melaena

The name pilot whale comes from European fishermen who believed there were herring under these whales and used them to guide their boats.

Description: This whale has a high, bulging forehead; a high, triangular, recurved back fin located forward of the center of the body; long, slender, pointed flippers; and protruding lips.

They are generally black or charcoal gray, sometimes with a narrow white stripe extending from the throat to belly. There is a dark gray blaze behind the eyes extending upward for several inches.

Males are much larger than females. Adults range from 11.8 to 27.9 feet long.

Distribution: Pilot whales are found in all oceans except the polar seas. There have been a number of strandings along the New England coast, including 3,000 beached on Cape Cod in 1874.

Behavior: They have a strong herd instinct and seem to get security from touching one another. They seem to follow a leader, and will follow it in the face of danger.

Pilot whales make a variety of sounds from a high-pitched squeal to a long belch.

They migrate between warm and cold waters with the seasons, travel up to 6 knots an hour, and dive for up to five minutes. They may thrash the water with their flukes when feeding. They feed mainly on squid but also take fish and small invertebrates.

The breeding season is May to November, and gestation takes 15 to 16 months. The calves are about 6 feet long at birth. They become weaned at 22 months, and may live to 50 years.

Harbor Porpoise
Phocoena phocoena

Harbor porpoises commonly enter bays, inlets and river mouths, where they may become stranded.

Description: Rather stocky in build, the harbor porpoise has a small, cone-shaped head. The snout is blunt and rounded. The back fin is low and triangular, located behind the middle of the body. The flippers are moderately long, and the flukes are broad.

The back, dorsal fin, flippers, and flukes are dark gray, greenish brown or nearly black. The undersides are white. There usually is a zone of light gray between back and belly. There may be a black stripe from the corners of the mouth to the flippers. Some are all black, but albinos are rare.

Distribution: They are common in the North Atlantic and eastern North Pacific. They are uncommon in New England waters.

HARBOR PORPOISE

Behavior: They may travel in pairs or in herds of 100 or more. They usually swim just below the surface, rising to breathe about four times a minute. They make clicking sounds at repetition rates as great as 1,000 per second. Most of their food is fish. They are known to dive to 165 feet.

The breeding season is late June to early August. Calving is in June or July. The newborn are 32 to 36 inches long.

These are the smallest members of the Cetacean family. They are 4 to 6 feet long and weigh 65 to 110 pounds.

Baleen Whales

These whales have paired nostrils, relatively large mouths, and no functional teeth when adult. Instead they have a series of flat, flexible, horny plates—called baleen or whalebone—that hang down from the roof of the mouth, the edges frayed into long bristles used to filter food from the water. As they move through water rich with tiny crustaceans, they draw water into their mouths and, with a large fleshy tongue, force it back through the baleen fringes, separating out the food, which is swallowed.

This group of whales is in the suborder Mysticeti which includes two families found in New England, the Balaenopteridae, or rorquals, and the Balaenidae, or right whales.

Rorquals

The rorquals, or fin-back whales, are a family which includes the largest animal in the world, the blue whale. They are long, slender and streamlined, with a pointed snout and a small dorsal fin usually located far back on the body. They have many grooves on the throat and belly and short baleen plates with bristly fringes. They feed on dense shoals of plankton, small shrimplike animals, and small fish.

Fin Whale
Balaenoptera physalus

Fin whales were once plentiful in New England waters and were hunted along the coast.

Description: They are the second largest and slenderest of the rorquals. They can be distinguished from other members of the family by the color of their baleen. The front one-half to one-third of the right baleen plates are bright yellowish white, while the left side plates and the greater part of the right are dark gray-blue. All the bristles are brownish gray. The lower jaw is white on the right side and blackish on the left. The number of baleen plates varies from 350 to 360 on one side of the jaw.

The number of grooves or pleats in the throat varies from 50 to 80. These extend to the navel.

The back is brownish black, fading into white on the belly. Some are yellow to green in appearance because of plankton which may cling to the skin. There are 2 dark areas passing from the flipper toward the pleats. A black stripe runs from the middle of the flanks to the anus. Two pale stripes extend from the blowhole to form a V along the back and upper sides. There are small white spots along the belly. The flippers and flukes are gray above and white below.

Females are slightly larger than males. They grow to at least 62 feet long and weigh about 50 tons.

Distribution: Fin whales are cosmopolitan but are rarely found in tropical waters or pack ice.

Behavior: Fin whales travel singly, in pairs, or in groups of 20 or more. During migration or at prime feeding grounds they may be in groups of 100 or more. Sometimes they become stranded along the coast or at the mouths of rivers.

Generally, fin whales migrate in the fall and spring. They appear in large numbers in the Gulf of Maine in early March, and they approach the southern coast of Newfoundland in early June, heading back south in October.

Fin whales swim steadily at 7 to 9 knots but when alarmed can hit 13 knots for short distances. They are strong and have been known to tow a whale ship at 2 to 3 knots.

When a fin whale breaks surface after a long dive of up to 20 minutes, the top of the head and blow hole usually emerge first. After surfacing the animal first spouts and then makes four to seven shallow dives. The spout may reach 20 feet into the air.

When feeding they swim on one side with their mouths open.

Fin whales are considered to take only one mate and are very affectionate towards each other. Breeding may take place year round. Gestation is 11 to 12 months, and the female usually has one young every other year. Fin whales are 20 to 21 feet long at birth, and the calf is nursed for six months. They are assumed to live 90 to 100 years.

FIN WHALE

Sei Whale

Balaenoptera borealis

Sei whales are known as skimmers because they feed slowly near the surface.

Description: The sei whale has a relatively large back fin; the flippers are rather small. The number of throat grooves varies between 30 and 60, and they do not extend much beyond the flippers. The number of baleen plates on one side of the whalebone varies from 219 to 402.

The back and flanks are bluish gray, the throat and belly whitish. The white may be expanded on the throat, narrowed in front of the flippers, and expanded again toward the rear. The flanks and sometimes the head have light spots. The flippers and flukes are dark gray above, lighter below. The whalebone is bluish black with white bristles.

Females are larger than males. Adults average 42 to 51 feet long.

Distribution: Sei whales are found in all oceans but prefer warmer waters than the fin or blue whale. They are rare in New England waters.

SEI WHALE

Behavior: They migrate as far north as sub-arctic waters in spring or early summer and south to subtropical waters in fall or winter. They are usually seen singly or in pairs, but groups of 50 or more have been reported.

Sei whales are among the fastest whales and can reach speeds of 26 knots. They can jump clear of the water. They breathe two or three times between soundings. Their primary food is tiny copepods.

They breed from November to March in the North Atlantic. The gestation period is about 12 months, and the newborn are about 12 feet long.

Minke Whale
Balaenoptera acutorostrata

Minke whales prefer in-shore waters, where they chase fish and sometimes get tangled in nets. They like to follow ships and sometimes lift their heads into the air to look around.

Description: The smallest baleen whale, the minke has a white band running across the flippers. The whalebone is cream white. The body is slender and the snout sharply pointed. The back fin has a broad base and is high, located on the back third of the body. There are about 50 throat grooves. The baleen plates are yellowish white and about 8 inches long.

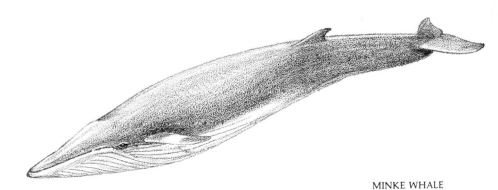

MINKE WHALE

These whales are blackish gray above, white below. A broad, light, crescent-shaped band runs from near the blowhole to the base of the flippers. The flippers and flukes are whitish below. Females are larger than males, ranging from 15 to 29 feet long.

Distribution: They are found in all oceans from the ice pack to the subtropics.

Behavior: Minke whales are seen singly or in pairs except on feeding grounds. Usual swimming speed is 8 to 10 knots. The spout may reach 7 feet high. They feed on a variety of fish and also eat some squid and crustaceans.

The breeding season extends over several winter months, and birth is in early winter. At birth they are nearly 10 feet long, and they nurse for 6 months.

Blue Whale
Balaenoptera musculus

The blue whale is the largest animal that ever lived. The largest ever killed was 109 feet long. A blue whale 80 feet long weighed 89.3 tons.

Description: The blue whale has a broad-snouted head, with a distinct ridge from the blowhole to the nose. The flippers are pointed and greatly curved. The back fin is very small. There are about 90 throat pleats that extend to the navel.

These whales are dark blue throughout, except for the tips and undersides of the flippers and flukes. The back, sides, and belly are mottled with light spots. Sometimes this species is called the "sulphur bottom " whale after the yellowish film of algae that occasionally forms on the undersides. The baleen is bluish black or black.

Females are larger than males. Adults average 51 to 88 feet.

Distribution: They inhabit all oceans, although their northern limit is the edge of the ice pack. They are rare on the east coast of the United States.

BLUE WHALE

Behavior: Blue whales migrate north in spring and early summer and head south in the fall to breed and calve. They swim singly, in pairs, or in groups of 2 or 3. They are loyal to their mates, and whale hunters said that to capture a pair of them they had to kill the female first, for the male would stay with her; a female, though, would not stand by a slain male.

They swim at about 10 knots but can hit 15 knots or more. Blue whales often follow ships. When they surface from sounding, they first expose the top of the head and blowhole. They may stay under for up to 20 minutes. The spout may go 50 feet into the air.

Blue whales are relatively shallow feeders. Their diet consists primarily of masses of small shrimplike creatures called "krill."

Breeding takes place in warmer waters, mostly in winter. Gestation takes 10 to 12 months. At birth they are about 23 feet long. They nurse for about 7 months, until the calf is about 52 feet long. They live about 90 years.

Whales, Dolphins, and Porpoises   139

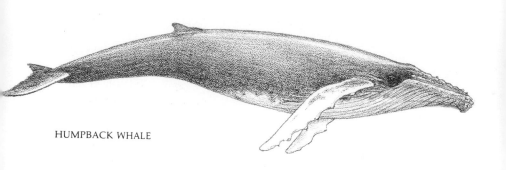

HUMPBACK WHALE

Humpback Whale
Megaptera novaeangliae

Humpbacks are playful. They like to jump clear of the water, often waving their long flippers. They roll on the surface, slapping it with their flukes. They turn somersaults above and below the water and will thrash the surface into foam with their flukes. At times they will swim on their backs for short periods.

Description: A stocky whale, the humpback has long, narrow flippers, knobbed on the forward edges. The back edges of the flukes have notches. There are wartlike round bumps on the head, forward of the blowhole. The dorsal fin is small. There are 270 to 400 baleen plates on each side of the mouth. There are about 25 throat grooves that reach from the chin to the navel. Usually there are barnacles on the chin, the front grooves and the front edges of the flippers, and on the flukes.

Humpback whales are usually black above and white below, with flippers white above but possibly spotted with black, or all black. The flukes are usually black, with white spots along back edges. The baleen may be brownish black or grayish black.

Females are larger than males. Adults range from 38 to 49 feet long and weigh an average of 29 tons.

Distribution: Humpbacks are found in nearly all oceans. In the

North Atlantic they range from arctic to tropic regions. They are seen fairly often in New England waters.

Behavior: They migrate to summer feeding grounds in polar regions and to winter breeding grounds in the tropics. They are reported to pass New England waters in April and May, going north, and October through December heading south.

Humpbacks travel singly, in pairs, and in groups of up to 12. They swim at 5 or 6 knots and can hit 12 knots. Wounded humpbacks have been known to hit 17 knots. They have tight social groups, and males will stand by injured females. They have been known to follow ships.

Usually, humpbacks dive for 6 to 7 minutes, but they have been known to stay under for 15. They make loud, short whistles, and wheezes. They make a series of varied sounds or "singing" for a period of 7 to 30 minutes, then repeat the pattern accurately. Each humpback seems to have its own song.

In the North Atlantic their primary food is minute crustaceans, but they occasionally eat fish.

The breeding season is year-long, and they show a lot of affection toward each other while breeding, stroking each other with flippers. Gestation is 11 to 12 months, and they are born 13 to 16 feet long. They live to be about 48 years old.

Right Whales

Members of this whale family include the bowhead, the right whale and the pigmy right whale. They have enormous heads and huge arched mouths with long baleen plates. These whales are slow swimmers and are found alone or in small groups. Right whales are the only members of this family found in New England waters.

Right Whale
Eubalaena glacialis

This whale was given its name by the whale hunters because it was the "right" whale: slow swimming, buoyant when killed, and yielding great amounts of oil.

RIGHT WHALE

Description: The right whale has a large head, about one-third its body length, a curved mouth, no back fin, no throat grooves, and a "bonnet" made of wartlike layers of skin infested by a parasitic crustacean.

The bonnet is on the snout, and other growths are found around the eyes, blowhole and along the lower jaw. The huge mouth is greatly curved. The lower lips are large and fleshy, scalloped along the upper margin. Some have horny bumps on the chin. The flippers are large, broad and somewhat pointed. The flukes are very broad and separated by a notch. There are 250 to 390 olive-black baleen plates on each side.

Right whales are usually black all over, but the belly may be white or white-spotted.

They average 35 to 45 feet long. A 56 foot whale weighed 148, 269 pounds.

Distribution: Right whales are found between 20°N and 70°N and between 20°S and 50°S. In New England waters they are present in spring as they migrate north and again in autumn as they migrate south.

Behavior: They swim singly, in pairs, and in groups of 25 or more. They often lie quietly on top of the water with the bonnet and blowhole protruding high in the air. Their usual migration speed is 2 to 3 knots, but they can hit 6 knots. Right whales may dive for 50 minutes. They spout five or six times in succession, then remain underwater 10 to 20 minutes. The spout may reach 15 feet high. The two jets diverge sideways like a V.

The right whale is a skimmer that feeds as it moves slowly along with its mouth open. The small crustaceans known as "krill" are its main food.

Breeding has been observed from February to April. The females calve once every 2 years after a gestation of about 12 months. The calf is nursed for about a year, and the females have strong motherly instincts.

7. Meat Eaters

THE CARNIVORES or meat eaters, cover a wide range in appearance, size and behavior. Most of them are land and woods animals, but some spend part or most of their time in water. Some are solitary, some live in pairs, and others hunt in groups. The order Carnivora includes scavengers and hunters. Their young are born helpless and are carefully cared for by their mothers, and sometimes by both parents.

Carnivore teeth are specially adapted to eating meat. The canines are large, round and pointed for grabbing and stabbing prey. Other teeth are shaped for cutting and tearing flesh.

They have worldwide distribution, excepting some ocean islands.

Coyotes, Wolves and Foxes

These three familiar predators are in the family called Canidae. They are doglike, muscular, deep-chested and long-legged. They have long muzzles and large, erect ears. Their tails are long and bushy.

Canids are very intelligent, alert and cunning. They are active year-round. The family is cosmopolitan, except for Antarctica.

Coyote
Canis latrans

Coyotes are opportunists and eat a wide variety of living and dead animals. They are masters at avoiding humans.

Description: The coyote has erect, pointed ears and a bushy, drooping tail. It has a long, narrow, pointed muzzle, a small, rounded nose, and eyes with a yellow iris. The front foot has five toes, the first small but with a strong claw. The hind foot has five toes. Females have ten nipples.

The fur is dense, long and coarse. Males and females look alike. Color varies greatly but is usually gray to cinnamon gray. The upper parts are a mix of buff-gray and black, with more blackish down the middle. The underparts are buff, mixed with deep gray and a few blackish hairs on the throat. The forefeet are blackish on top. The muzzle is brownish, sometimes nearly cinnamon brown. The forehead and cheeks are paler, mixed with gray and black. The crown is tawnier, becoming reddish tawny or brown on the nape and the back of the ears. The chin is grayish. The tail is colored like the back on top, with black at the base and tip, and paler below.

An annual molt starts in June and is completed in the fall. Albino and black coyotes are rare.

Coyotes are closely related to and can crossbreed with wolves and dogs. Careful skull examination is needed to definitely tell the species apart. New England coyotes are known to contain some wolf genes, and it has been suggested that they be officially known as *canis latrans var.* and popularly called eastern coyotes. "Coydog" is the common name of a cross between a dog and a coyote.

Males are slightly larger than females. Adults are from 44.9 to 52 inches long, with a tail 11.4 to 15.4 inches long and a hind foot 6.7 to 8.7 inches long. Large males reach 50 pounds.

Distribution: Originally found in the open plains of the United States, the coyote is found from Alaska south through the western United States to Central America. Within the past 50 years it has expanded into the northeastern United States and Canada. It is found in all the New England states, with the possible exception of Rhode Island.

Ecology: In the East, coyotes live in brushy country bordering second growth hardwood forests, fields mixed with thickets, and marshlands. They sleep on the ground but make a den for pups. The den is concealed in a brushy slope, steep bank, rocky ledge, under a stump, hollow log, log pile, deserted building, or in dry culvert. They will dig dens but prefer to enlarge the burrows of woodchucks, foxes, skunks, or rabbits. Some dens go straight back, while others go straight down 2 to 4 feet. They are up to 30 feet long and may have several entrances concealed in vegetation. The den chamber is about 3 feet in diameter. The den is not lined but the adults keep it clean. After the pups are born, small balls of fur from the female's abdomen may be found at the den entrance.

Man and dogs are their chief predators. They have ticks, mites, lice and internal parasites. They are susceptible to distemper, mange, tularemia, rabies and heartworms.

Behavior: Chiefly nocturnal, coyotes may be seen at dusk and dawn. They are social animals, and may be seen in pairs or in groups of three or more when hunting. They have keen sight, hearing and smell.

When hunting together coyotes normally travel single file, often on the packed runways of hares or deer, and they have their own runways which they mark with scent posts by urinating.

They seem to howl for pleasure and to call to warn other coyotes. The adults have two basic sounds, the bark and a flat howl. In groups they "yip-yip," warble, laugh, and give short and irregular howls. Young coyotes scream and gargle.

COYOTE

Home range may be 5 miles in diameter in summer and as much as 25 square miles in winter. Coyotes usually trot but gallop when pressed. They run as fast as 30 miles an hour and possibly as fast as 43 miles an hour for a short distance. They are strong swimmers.

When stalking rabbits and other small animals coyotes creep up for some distance, freeze like a pointing dog, then pounce. Two or more coyotes may chase an animal in relays. They usually attack from the front and bite the prey in the throat. They often bury surplus food.

Deer carrion is thought to be their main food in New England, but coyotes also prey on fawns. They eat birds, snakes, frogs, lizards, turtles, fishes, crayfish, and insects, as well as fruits, berries, and other plants.

Some pairs may stay together for several years, but usually for just one season. In the northern part of their range, coyotes breed mainly in February. The pups are born 60 to 65 days after mating, with four to eight pups in the litter. (Litters have been recorded with up to 19 pups.) At birth they are blind and helpless, covered with short woolly hair, weighing a half pound. The eyes open at 10 to 14 days. They are nursed for 2 weeks, and about the time their eyes open they are fed partly digested food regurgitated by the parents. They emerge from the den at 3 to 4 weeks and are weaned at 9 weeks. After weaning they leave the den area, but the family stays together until early fall.

Red Fox
Vulpes vulpes

A red fox could easily be mistaken for a small collie except for the fur color, which is brighter.

Description: The muzzle is long and pointed. The ears are large, pointed, erect and well-furred. The coat is dense and soft. The tail is long, round and bushy, and carried upright. The legs are fairly long, and the feet are small, with five toes on the front and four in the back. Females have eight nipples.

Males and females have the same coloration. They are bright yellowish red on the sides to deep yellowish brown on the back, darkest in the middle of the back and shoulders. The rump is grizzled to dull white. The face and neck are dusky. The nose,

RED FOX

backs of the ears, legs and feet are black. The front of the ears, cheeks and throat, and the middle of the belly are white. The tail is reddish, mixed with black hairs, and the tip is white.

Color phases include the cross fox, which has much more black on the legs and in the underfur; the silver fox, which is black with white-tipped guard hairs; the black or melanistic fox; the samson fox, with only woolly underfur; and the bastard fox, which has much more black hair on the belly and legs and has a smoky appearance. Albino fox are rare.

Males are larger than females. Adults are 35.5 to 41.4 inches long, with a tail 12.6 to 15.8 inches long and the hind foot 5.5 to 7.1 inches long. They average 8 to 12 pounds, but may reach 17 pounds.

Distribution: Red foxes are found over most of North America from Baffin Island, Canada, and Alaska to the the southern United States, except for coastal western Canada, Oregon and California, the Great Plains, the southwestern desert, and the extreme southeast.

Ecology: Red foxes are found in a wide variety of habitats but avoid open, brushless plains and dense forests. They prefer sparsely settled open country with cover, such as farmlands. They follow regular routes across low, rolling hills, valleys, ravines, marshes, streams, through swamps and along waterways.

They may dig their own dens but they prefer to enlarge a woodchuck or other mammal's den. Dens are found in wooded areas in banks, gullies, and fencerows, under logs or abandoned buildings, and on level ground where digging is easy and drainage good. The chamber is merely a widening of the burrow, usually lined with grass for the pups. Sometimes there are extra chambers where food is stored or where the pups can be moved when there is danger. The den is kept clean but the entrances are littered with bones and food parts.

The den is at least 4 feet underground in a complex tunnel system 25 to 75 feet long. There may be several entrances, 8 inches wide and 15 inches high, usually facing south.

Man and dogs are the foxes' main predators, though great horned owls are known to take unwary pups. They are susceptible to rabies outbreaks. They have fleas and ticks, and suffer from a number of diseases including distemper, heartworms, tularemia, rickets, mange and septicemia. They also have internal parasites.

Behavior: Red foxes sleep outside, even in sub-zero weather, and use the den mainly for pups or as refuge. They are chiefly night hunters but may be seen hunting mice at dawn and dusk. They prefer the solitary life except during denning season. Their senses of smell, sight and hearing are keen.

They make a short "yap, yap" and a combination of long howls, screeches and yells.

Red foxes are strong trotters and can hit 26 miles an hour for short distances. They usually circle and backtrack to avoid dogs.

When hunting, a red fox often trots back and forth with nose to ground, or it may crouch low, scarcely moving. When prey is scented, the fox pauses for several seconds and then, with a spring, rush or pounce, seizes its prey and kills it with powerful jaws. Red foxes are good swimmers. They sometimes wash themselves by licking their fur but will also roll in rotting carcasses.

Sometimes red foxes are friendly to other animals. They have been known to play with dogs, to walk with mountain sheep, to run among caribou and to live in burrows with woodchucks.

Their home range is less than 5 miles in diameter. The young will usually move over 5 miles from the area they were born in.

Red foxes are opportunists and will eat anything readily available, including carrion. They feed on small mammals, birds, eggs, insects, worms, turtles and their eggs, frogs and snakes, wild berries, grapes, plums, apples, nuts, corn and other grains. Sometimes they eat rope, twine, paper, sticks and trash. They normally bury surplus food or cover it with grass or leaves, sprinkling it with urine.

The breeding season is from mid-January to late February. The gestation averages 53 days, and litters have one to ten pups born in late March or early April. As many as five litters have been found within 200 acres. Red foxes may mate for life.

At birth red fox pups are blind and helpless, covered with fine, dense hair. The eyes open about the 9th day. The pups remain in the den until 4 or 5 weeks old. They play about the den entrance with bones, feathers, skin and leftover food. They are weaned at about 12 weeks.

Gray Fox

Urocyon cincreoargenteus

Gray foxes are skillful tree climbers. They climb fast by shinnying up the trunk to a limb. They will jump from limb to limb and climb trees to hunt prey or escape dogs.

Description: The gray fox is smaller than the red fox, with a shorter muzzle and legs. The long, black-tipped tail is bushy and has a mane of short, stiff black hairs. The claws on the front feet are more curved to aid in tree climbing.

Males and females look alike, and have coarse, dense fur. The back is grizzled gray from a mixture of black and white bands on the black-tipped guard hairs. The sides of the neck, back of the ears, a band across the chest, the inner and back surfaces of the legs, the feet, the sides of the belly, and the bottom of the tail are reddish brown. The cheeks, throat, inner ears and the greater part of the belly are white. The nose and chin are black. The muzzle and rims around the eyes are blackish. The tail is black above, reddish brown below.

Only one albino gray fox has been recorded, but there are black variants. They molt in the summer.

Gray foxes measure 35.5 to 41 inches long, with the tail 11.8 to

Meat Eaters   151

15.4 inches and the hind foot 5.1 to 5.9 inches. They weigh 7 to 13 pounds but have been recorded to 19 pounds.

Distribution: Gray foxes are found from southern Canada throughout the United States, except in Montana, Idaho, Wyoming and most of Washington. The species ranges into Mexico and Central America. These foxes are found in all the New England states, but only rarely in the southern most portions of Maine.

Ecology: The gray fox is a forest hunter, living in rough, rocky areas in dense hardwood and hardwood-softwood forests, swamps, thickets and briers with nearby water and lots of cover for hunting and hiding.

These animals rarely dig a den and do not use a burrow often, but will have a series of dens concealed in dense cover under logs, in tree and stump cavities, in rock crevices or caves, under abandoned buildings, in brush, or in sawmill piles. The den may be lined with leaves, grass, fur, bark or other soft material.

Man and dogs are their chief predators, but bobcats, large hawks, and the great horned owl sometimes catch pups. They suffer from heartworms, rabies, distemper, mange, listeriosis, tularemia, fleas, ticks, lice and internal parasites.

Behavior: Secretive and shy, gray foxes are night hunters but sometimes forage in daytime. They can run to 26 miles an hour.

Their voice is similar to that of the red fox, but louder, and they bark and yap less often. Their home range is variable from less than a mile wide in denning season to over 5 miles in the fall.

They eat a wide variety of small mammals, birds, eggs, frogs, snakes, turtles, insects, corn, berries, grapes, apples, acorns, and carrion.

Gray foxes breed from mid-January to May. Gestation lasts 51 to 63 days, with litters of two to seven. At birth they are blind and helpless and almost hairless. They are weaned at 8 to 10 weeks.

Bears

The bears, members of the family Ursidae, are the largest land-based meat eaters in North America. They seem sluggish and walk with a shuffle, but are also agile and can walk on their hind feet. Bears are usually solitary wanderers and peaceful but can be ferocious when provoked.

Black Bear

Ursus americanus

The black bear is the largest meat-eating animal in New England, reaching weights of 600 pounds or more. When born, however, bear cubs may weigh half a pound or less.

Description: Black bears are heavy animals with short, rounded ears, a furry, short tail, a long muzzle, and a nearly straight face profile. Their broad front feet each have five toes with short claws, as do the rear feet. The females have six nipples.

The coat is thick, long and fairly soft. Males and females look alike. The normal color is glossy black or brownish black all over, except for the muzzle, which is tan. They usually have a small white patch on the throat. Some black bears are brown and cinnamon or blue. Albino black bears are rare. They begin an annual molt in April or May and complete it in October.

Males are slightly larger than females. Adults are 50 to 70.1 inches long, with a tail 3.1 to 5.1 inches long and a hind foot 7.5 to 11 inches long.

Distribution: Once found over most of North America, the black bear has been eliminated from most of the north central and central United States. In New England it is found in the wilder woodland areas. Black bears are fairly common in most of Maine, northern and central New Hampshire and Vermont. The species occurs in western Massachusetts and northwestern Connecticut but probably not Rhode Island.

Ecology: Black bears are found in forested wilderness and swamps, preferring mixed stands of hard and softwoods, usu-

BLACK BEAR

ally with brushy undergrowth near streams, ponds and lakes. The winter den might be in a hollow log, cave, rocky ledge, under fallen trees, in a root cavity, in brush, under windfalls, slash, or in a drainage culvert. Sometimes the den is lined with bark, leaves, grasses or moss.

Man and dogs are their chief predators. Males of all ages are most vulnerable because they move around more and are less wary. They have fleas, ticks, lice and internal parasites, but seem disease resistant.

Behavior: Mostly night animals, black bears sometimes hunt during the day. They are alert and wary and remain close to cover. They rarely attack man except when wounded or cornered or with cubs. Except for females with cubs, they are solitary. When two bears meet they usually avoid contact but may threaten each other.

Black bears have an awkward, shuffling gait but can run up to 32 miles an hour. They sometimes stand on their hind feet to look around. They drink a lot and enjoy bathing and wallowing in warm weather. They are strong swimmers and expert tree climbers. They may climb a tree to get nuts or honey or just to relax and nap.

Generally silent, black bears have no regular call sounds. At times they may "woof" or growl, and in stress they bellow. Injured bears bawl and sob like humans, and females with cubs make low grunts, huffs, mumbles and squeaks. Cubs squall when hungry or frightened and whimper when lost. They purr when happy.

Black bears spend a lot of time wandering. Females with cubs tend to have restricted home ranges, while males move about widely, particularly during the breeding season. In their home territories bears use regular trails, and these trails may be marked by "bear trees": to mark these, the bears stand on their hind legs, and, reaching as high as possible, they claw and bite the bark. Both males and females mark trees, and the reason is not clearly understood.

Black bears are not true hibernators but go into a deep sleep in winter, with their heart beat, breathing and body temperature only slightly reduced. Females give birth to and nurse their cubs in mid-winter.

Black bears get very fat in the fall in preparation for the winter sleep. They usually den when a sufficient layer of fat has been accumulated, without regard to weather. Females usually den first. They appear to be in good condition when they awake in the spring, usually in March or April, but lose weight rapidly in the next few weeks.

Black bears will eat almost anything, including dead bears. They eat grubs, larvae, insects, seeds, berries, grapes, apples, acorns, beechnuts, hardwood leaves, frogs, reptiles, mice, fish, carrion, and garbage. They are fond of sweets and raid bee hives and the food stores of campers. They will rip open rotten tree stumps for ants and their eggs.

Female black bears, called sows, usually breed once every two years. Breeding season peaks about mid-June. The cubs are born 7 to 7½ months after breeding in litters of one to five, with the usual number two.

Newborn cubs weigh 6 to 12 ounces, with eyes and ears closed and with a coat of fine, soft, mottled gray hair. They are generally uncoordinated until about 46 days old, and they begin to walk at two months. The eyes open at about a month.

The female is very protective of her cubs, and they are weaned when about 7 months old. Cubs leave the den at about 3 months. They will remain with the female until the second summer of their lives. Bears live to 25 years in the wild.

Raccoons

Raccoons, ringtails, kinkajous and coatis are all in a family called Procyonidae. They have medium to long bushy tails, usually with alternating light and dark rings. The legs have five flexible toes for climbing trees.

They are both plant and animal eaters—omnivorous—and spend a lot of time in trees. They have keen senses of smell, hearing and vision. They may be solitary or live in family groups.

As a family they are exclusively American animals, except for the pandas.

Raccoon
Procyon lotor

The second half of the raccoon's scientific name, lotor, means "the washer," referring to it's supposed habit of always washing food before it eats it. The fact is, away from water raccoons eat food wherever they find it.

Description: A robust animal, the raccoon has a black mask across the eyes and cheeks and a round, bushy tail which is ringed. The legs are long and slender. The feet have five long toes and claws. The head is broad with a pointed muzzle, large pointed ears and dark eyes.

The coat is long and thick. Males and females look alike. The fur is dark brown at the base and the hairs are banded black, with lighter rings of gray or yellowish gray and black. The back color varies from dull iron gray, to brownish, to blackish, to buff or yellow on the neck and tail. The sides are grayer and paler.

The underparts are thinly overlaid with long grayish or buff guard hairs which only partly cover dense dull brownish or yellowish gray underfur. The top of the head is grizzled. The sides of the muzzle, the lips and chin are white. The throat is dark grayish brownish black. The tops of the feet are yellowish white. The tail is alternately banded with five to seven rings, brownish black alternating with yellowish gray· and ending a black tip. Albino, black, white, chestnut and red raccoons are seen but rarely.

Males tend to be larger than females. They measure from 28.4 to 36.2 inches long, with a tail 8.6 to 10.2 inches and hind foot 3.9 to 5.1 inches long. They weigh 9 to 26 pounds.

Distribution: Raccoons are found from most of southern Canada through most of the United States except high portions of the Rocky Mountains and the arid southwest, and through Mexico to Panama.

Ecology: Raccoons prefer fairly open mature hardwood areas with mature hardwood trees near streams, rivers, ponds and lakes. They generally nest in hollow trees but will use hollow logs, stump cavities, rock crevices, caves, old mines, deserted buildings, barn lofts, cornshocks, haystacks, slab piles, brush piles, tile drains, culverts, abandoned beaver houses, muskrat houses, fox dens and woodchuck burrows. They may have more than one den, and the same dens are used year after year.

Man and dogs are their chief enemies. Bobcats, coyotes, fishers, and great horned owls capture cubs. They suffer from ticks, lice, fleas, internal parasites and a variety of diseases including distemper, pneumonia, trichinosis, tuberculosis and rabies.

Behavior: Primarily night animals, raccoons are also seen at daytime. They den during winter but do not hibernate and are active in mild winters. They live off fat deposits during the winter, losing about 50% of their body weight before they resume feeding in the spring.

Raccoons tend to be solitary, except for pairs and families. The size of their home range depends on food supplies, age and sex of the animal, and the weather. One raccoon was reported to travel 165 miles in 164 days.

They have well-developed senses of hearing, sight and touch but not so keen senses of taste and smell. They are curious and clever, and have good memories. They make many sounds including low purrs, grunts, growls, snarls, shrill screams, twitters, whimpers and squeals.

Raccoons have an ambling pace, a trot and a run. They can run to 15 miles an hour. They are good swimmers and if chased into water by dogs will sometimes turn and attack a dog by climbing on its head. They are strong and courageous and will fight a dog their own size. On land they usually fight by lying on their backs and slashing with their teeth.

They are expert climbers and come down from a tree either head or tail first.

Raccoons are opportunists and will eat both animal and plant foods of all kinds.

They are promiscuous in mating. They breed from late January to the middle of March, with a gestation period of about 63 days. The litter has three to seven cubs, averaging four. At birth they weigh 2.6 ounces, have fur and grow rapidly. The eyes open at about 19 days; they are weaned by 16 weeks and may start eating solid food at 9 weeks. The female usually keeps her young in a hollow tree for 50 to 60 days and then moves them to the ground, usually to a wetland. They live to 6 years in the wild.

Weasels

The Mustelidae, or weasel family, is a surprising group because of the diversity of its members, from the agile fisher to the water-loving otter to the clumsy skunk.

Some of these animals are fierce, while other species are gentle. They live in a great variety of habitats from woods to water. They are short-legged but have great strength and endurance.

They are worldwide in distribution except for Antarctica and most oceanic islands.

Marten

Martes americana americana

Description: Two-thirds the size of a house cat, the marten is lithe and long with short legs, a small, triangular head, large, rounded ears, and long, bushy tail. Each foot has five toes with semirectractile claws, and the soles are densely furred. Females have six nipples.

Males and females look alike. The fur is thick, soft and lustrous. Color varies a lot from animal to animal, mostly browns and yellow oranges. The general color is rich yellowish to light brown on the back mixed with blackish brown hairs, darker on the legs, feet and tail. The underparts are cinnamon. The head is grayish brown to almost white, darkest on the nose and ears,

MARTEN

which are edged with white. The throat and chest have irregular patches of bright reddish orange. Color phases include light yellow, silver-sprinkled, nearly white, slate and almost all black. They have a single annual molt that begins in late summer and is complete by late October.

Males are larger than females. Adults are 20 to 26 inches long, with a tail 5.9 to 9 inches long and a hind foot 2.8 to 3.9 inches. They weigh from 1.5 to 3.5 pounds.

Distribution: Once found over much of northern north America, the marten has now been greatly reduced in range and numbers, especially in the south. It is fairly abundant in northern Maine and present in limited numbers in southern Maine and northern New Hampshire. It probably occurs in remote parts of Vermont and Massachusetts.

Ecology: Cool, dense forests of northern spruce, balsam and hemlock in mountainous regions are favored by martens; they are also found in mixed hardwood-softwood forests. Dens are usually found in hollow trees, under logs and stumps, and sometimes in rock crevices.

Man is their chief predator. Some martens are caught by fishers, lynx, bobcats and great horned owls. They have fleas, mites, lice, scabies and internal parasites.

Behavior: Martens do not hibernate, although they might hole up or move to lower elevations in winter. They are wanderers and do not seem to have a permanent den.

Active night and day, martens are secretive, bold, energetic, fearless, alert, quick and curious. They are mostly solitary except during breeding season and when females have young. Usually silent when angry or trapped, they can snarl, hiss, scream, screech and growl. They don't like water, and avoid it. They have well-developed senses of smell, sight and hearing.

Martens are good tree climbers. On the ground they investigate every nook and cranny, and capture prey by pouncing. They seem to enjoy jumping on snow. The home range is 12 to 15 square miles. They make scent posts by rubbing abdominal scent glands on the ground, rocks and branches both before and during the mating season.

Martens undergo population cycles based on a three-year rise and fall, apparently related to food shortages in part. Their main food is small mammals, and they are fond of red squirrels, chipmunks, flying squirrels, field mice, voles, shrews, moles, snowshoe hares, deer carrion and ruffed grouse. They also eat birds and their eggs, frogs, toads, fish, reptiles, insects and fruits.

Breeding in midsummer, martens are polygamous. The gestation period is between 259 and 275 days; implantation of the fertilized egg is delayed in the uterus until about 27 days before the female gives birth. The litters range from one to five young. They are born blind and helpless, covered with fine fur. Eyes open at 4 to 6 weeks, and the young are independent at 3 months old. They live to 6 years in the wild.

Fisher
Martes pennanti pennanti

Fisher is a poor choice of names for this large weasel, since about the only fish it eats are those it finds dead. It has a variety of other popular names, including black cat, fisher cat, pekan and black fox.

Description: The fisher is twice as large as the marten. The head is shaped like a wedge, with the muzzle somewhat pointed. The ears are broad and somewhat rounded. The neck, legs and feet are stout. The claws are strong and curved for climbing. The tail is long and bushy. They have large scent glands which produce a musky odor. The female has four nipples.

The coat is dense, long and glossy. Females tend to be darker than males. Older fishers have many white-tipped hairs on the shoulders and backs. The back is grayish brown or brownish black, lighter on the sides but darker on the rump. The underparts are brownish. The face, neck, and shoulders are frosted with gray and pale brown. The nose, legs and feet are blackish. The tail is usually all black. The ears have pale linings. There are a few white patches on the neck and throat. Color phases include white, black, fawn and mottled. They molt in late summer or early fall.

Males are much larger than females. Adults are from 31.5 to 40.2 inches long, with a tail 11.8 to 16.5 inches and the hind foot 3.5 to 5.5 inches. They weigh from 4.4 to 20.3 pounds.

Distribution: The fisher is found from southeastern Alaska and British Columbia to Hudson Bay and eastern Canada, south in the Adirondack Mountains of New York, northwestern Maine, the White Mountains of New Hampshire, the Green Mountains of Vermont, and probably in the Berkshires of Massachusetts; it is also found in the Rocky Mountains of Wyoming and the Sierra Nevada in California.

Ecology: Fishers prefer dense hardwood-softwood forests but are also found in open second growth stands and sometimes in recently burned over areas. They rarely dig burrows. They make their dens in tree hollows, logs, rocky ledges, under large boulders, in old porcupine dens, under brush piles or in the snow. The dens may be lined with leaves.

Man and possibly bobcats, lynxes and black bears prey on fishers. They have fleas, ticks, mites, mange and internal parasites.

Behavior: Fishers are active night and day all year but den during blizzards. They are solitary except for brief mating periods. They are as agile in trees as on the ground. When hunting they dart beneath logs or upturned stumps—almost any place prey might be found. They descend trees head first. Fishers are good swimmers and frequently take to the water.

Wary and usually irritable, they arch their backs like cats, show their teeth and growl, snarl, and hiss when bothered. In breeding season they grunt. Fishers are powerful and fierce, and can fight off a dog when cornered.

Fishers are great travelers. They forage along more or less straight routes, denning as they go. They seem to prefer to follow ridges, usually crossing small streams, to get to the next ridge. The normal home range is 8 to 15 miles in diameter, and they may travel 100 miles in 12 days in winter.

Fishers will eat whatever is available. They hunt by chance and generally do not try to run down or stalk prey. The only animal they hunt deliberately is the porcupine. Fishers kill porcupines by repeated attacks on the head; the porcupines die from a number of wounds. They eat the porcupine from the underside, where there are no quills, or from the head and neck, and when they finish leave a flat and remarkably clean porcupine skin, minus flesh and bones.

Contrary to popular belief, porcupine quills do often penetrate

FISHER

deeply into a fisher but seem to cause no festering or swelling. Most quills are passed through the fisher's digestive tract.

They also eat snowshoe hares, carrion, white-tailed deer, shrews, mice, squirrels, birds, amphibians, fish, insects, apples, and beechnuts.

The breeding season lasts from late February through April. Gestation is about 51 weeks long, since the fertilized egg is not implanted into the uterus for 9 or 10 months after mating. The kits are born in March or early April, in litters of one to four, blind, helpless and partially furred. They open their eyes about the 53rd day and depend on the female for 4 months or more.

Ermine

Mustela erminea cicognanii

Agile, fearless, cunning, the ermine is a tireless hunter and killer of much more than it can eat.

Description: A smaller version of the long-tailed weasel, the ermine has a long, slender body with a long neck and short legs. The head is small and triangular. The eyes are small and the ears low and rounded. There are five small clawed toes on each foot.

The tail is short and bushy and less than one-third the body length. Females have eight nipples.

The coat has a soft, short underfur and long, coarse, glossy guard hairs. Males and females look alike, and they have two distinct colors in winter and summer.

In summer the back is uniformly dark brown, slightly darker on the head and legs, becoming white at the feet. The upper lips are narrowly banded with white, and the chin and throat are whitish. The underparts are whitish to pale yellowish, the color extending down the sides of the legs and into the feet. The toes are often white-tipped. The last third of the brown tail is black, even in winter. The winter coat is white, tinged with yellow on the back and underparts. Albino ermine occur rarely.

Ermine molt in spring and autumn. The fall molt usually starts in October and is complete by late November. The spring molt begins about the middle of March and is complete by late April.

Males are larger than females. Adults are 7.5 to 11.8 inches long, with a tail 1.6 to 3.2 inches and a hind foot 1.6 to 3.2 inches. they weigh 1.6 to 3.7 ounces.

Distribution: Ermines are circumpolar in distribution. In North America they are found from Baffin Island and Southampton Island through most of Canada, south to Maryland and Minnesota; from western Montana south through the Rocky Mountains

ERMINE

to New Mexico; and from Alaska south to northern California.

Ecology: In the north, ermines live in low brush and thickets along waterways in large forested areas. In the southern part of their range they are found in brushland, open country with hedgerows or stone walls, in old buildings, and sometimes in swampy areas.

The den is a large, loose structure beneath a stone wall, rock pile, log, tree, hay pile or other hiding spot. There may be three or four tunnels leading to a den. The breeding nest is lined with grasses, fur, leaves and feathers.

Man, large hawks, owls, foxes, cats and large snakes prey on ermine. They have fleas and internal parasites.

Behavior: Active throughout the year, ermines are mostly night animals, although they sometimes hunt in daylight. When surprised they will duck into the nearest hiding spot, but a mouse-like squeak will bring them right back for a look. They have good hearing, smell, and sight. They have several calls including hisses, purrs, chatters, grunts and screeches. The female makes a high, reedy note when approached by a male. They stamp their feet when angry and will emit a musky scent from anal glands if greatly disturbed.

Ermines are fair swimmers and will chase prey in water. Their normal gait is a series of small bounds with the back arched. They can leap five or six feet and run to about 8 miles an hour. Normal home range is 30 to 40 acres but when food is scarce they may travel 2 or 3 miles a night.

Mostly ground animals, ermines also climb trees. They dart about while hunting and pause now and then to look around. They usually kill by biting the back of the skull, and they commonly kill more than they can eat. Ermines do not suck blood as is commonly believed but will lick it from the wound on the base of the skull or neck of their prey.

Ermines hunt and eat mice, voles, rats, rabbits, chipmunks, shrews, frogs, lizards, small snakes, birds, insects and earthworms. They eat carrion when hunting is poor.

Breeding season is in early summer. The young are born from mid-April to mid-May after a 9-month gestation. There is a delayed implantation of the fertilized egg into the uterus. Litters vary from four to nine. Newborns are blind and flesh-colored, with fine white hairs on the neck. Their eyes open at 35 days. At 7 weeks old the males are larger than their mothers. The male may help the female care for the young. Ermine have a life span of 5 to 6 years.

Long-tailed Weasel
Mustela freneta

Efficient and voracious hunters, long-tailed weasels strike at the base of the skull with their teeth while hugging the prey with their long body; this usually results in a quick kill.

Description: The long-tailed weasel is similar in appearance to the ermine, but is larger, with a longer tail. The feet have five slightly webbed toes, each with a small claw. Females have eight nipples.

The fur is rather short, moderately fine and not dense. Males and females look alike. In summer the back is uniformly dark brown, extending down onto the feet and toes. The underparts are yellowish white with occasional brown spots. The tail is brown and is tipped with black in both winter and summer. It is believed that this weasel only changes to white where winters are very cold, but one researcher found that only males remain brown in winter.

The autumn molt begins by mid-October and is complete by mid-November. The change from white to brown starts from mid-February to early March and is completed by mid-April.

Adult males are much larger than females. They measure 11.8 to 17.3 inches long, with a tail 3.2 to 6.3 inches and the hind foot 1.2 to 2 inches long. They weigh from 2.5 to 9.3 ounces.

Distribution: Long-tailed weasels are found from southern Canada to Peru. They are absent from the southwestern United States and northwestern Mexico, except for northern Baja California.

Ecology: Found from sea level to timberline, long-tailed weasels prefer open woodlands, brushlands, and fencerows in rocky areas near water. They seldom dig their own dens but enlarge the burrow of a chipmunk, a hole under a stump, a crevice, among

LONG-TAILED WEASEL

rocks in a stone wall or around abandoned buildings.

The nest is about 6 inches underground and about 2 feet from the burrow entrance. It is about 9 inches in diameter, may have up to four entrances, and may be lined with grass, mouse and shrew fur.

Man, dogs, coyotes, red foxes, large hawks and owls prey on long-tailed weasels. They have fleas, ticks, lice and internal parasites.

Behavior: Long-tailed weasels are active year-round and never stay in the den for long, regardless of weather conditions. They are mostly night animals.

Good swimmers, they can climb well and will chase a squirrel up a tree. They are generally solitary, but two may play together. They will attack a man or other animal which interferes with their hunting.

The size of the long-tailed weasel's home range seems to be variable, according to studies made by various scientists.

Long-tailed weasels prey on small mammals, bats, hares, rabbits, birds and their eggs, frogs, snakes, earthworms, insects and carrion.

They breed in July and August, and the young are born the next April or May following a gestation of 205 or 337 days as the result of delayed implantation of the fertilized egg in the uterus.

Newborns are blind, naked and pink with a few fine, white hairs over the back. The eyes open at about 36 days and the female starts to wean them at this time. They have been known to live 5 or more years in captivity.

Mink
Mustela vison

Restless and curious, some mink are bold enough to try to steal fish caught by fishermen.

Description: Mink are nearly as large as a house cat, though much thinner. The head is small, broad, and flattened, and tapers to a pointed muzzle. The neck is thick and muscular. The ears are short, low and rounded. The legs are short and stout. The feet each have five slightly webbed toes. The tail is long and bushy. They have well-developed anal scent glands. Females have six nipples.

MINK

The coat is thick and dense. The underfur is oily and overlaid with long, coarse, glistening guard hairs. Males and females are alike in coloring. The fur is nearly a uniform, rich dark brown, except for a white spot on the chest and belly. Color phases do not appear to occur in the wild, but mink farms have bred such color mutations as black, topaz, white, pastel, sapphire, platinum, silver-blue and amber-gold.

They molt twice a year, spring and fall.

Males are much larger than females. Adults range from 18.1 to 26.8 inches long, with a tail 6 to 9.5 inches long and a hind foot 2 to 3.1 inches long. They weigh 1.1 to 2.5 pounds.

Distribution: Mink are found throughout Alaska, most of Canada except the tundra regions, and throughout the United States, except for the desert region of the southwest.

Ecology: Mink live along streams, rivers, lakes and marshes, preferring forested, log-strewn areas. The den may be in a burrow along or near the banks of a water body, under a log or stump, in a rock recess, or in a muskrat house. A mink may dig its own burrow or take one over from another animal. The burrow may be 12 or more feet long and 1 to 3 feet below ground, with two to five entrances.

The birthing den is an enlargement of the burrow and is located a few feet from water's edge. The chamber is 12 inches in diameter and lined with grass, leaves, fur and feathers.

Man, dogs, red foxes, bobcats and great horned owls prey on mink. They have fleas, ticks, lice and internal parasites. Ranch mink develop many diseases but wild mink seem to be bothered only by tularemia and abscesses.

Behavior: Mostly nocturnal, mink also hunt at dusk and dawn. Active year-round, they will den during cold stormy weather. They are solitary except during breeding season and when females have young.

Mink travel by a series of bounds 10 to 20 inches long, with the back arched at each leap. They are alert and often rear up on their hind legs to look around. They climb on logs and stumps and may climb trees to escape danger. They like to push through the snow, and may slide down snow-covered slopes on their bellies.

Well-adapted to water, mink swim with most of the body submerged and move underwater with ease. They dive to 18 feet and swim underwater up to 100 feet. They are tireless wanderers and often cruise a wide range from one watershed to another when food is scarce or if their water freezes or dries up.

Mink are skillful hunters and will persistently trail their prey by scent. They are fighters and will attack animals larger than themselves. They usually kill by biting behind the skull. They prefer to drag prey to their den for eating, and they cache food.

They make purring grunts, loud growls, snarls, screams, and shrill screeches. Hearing and sight are not keen but smelling is highly developed. When excited or hurt mink spray liquid musk from their prominent anal glands.

Mink eat fish, frogs, crayfish, clams, turtles, snakes, lizards, earthworms, insects, mice, rats, bats, muskrats, moles, rabbits and birds. Occasionally they eat grass.

Mink are promiscuous, breeding from late February to early April. The litter of two to ten kits is born in April or May after gestation of 40 to 75 days, resulting from delayed implantation of the fertilized egg until 30 or 32 days before birth. At birth they are blind and helpless, covered with fine, short white hairs. The eyes open in about 25 days, and the kits are weaned in 5 or 6 weeks. The family remains together until August. Mink live to 3 to 6 years in the wild.

Striped Skunk
Mephitis mephitis nigra

It is a rare person who cannot instantly recognize the pungent odor of skunk musk. The fluid is a yellowish, oily, nauseating substance sometimes containing creamy yellow curds. The musk comes from a pair of oval anal glands which can be compressed so forcefully by muscles that the stinky substance can be fired 15 feet or more.

Description: About the size of a house cat, the striped skunk has a small head, short legs, wide rear end and bushy tail. The front feet have long, curved claws for digging. Each foot has five toes.

These animals have long thick coats with soft, wavy underfur and long, coarse, shiny guard hairs. Males and females look

STRIPED SKUNK

alike. The color is mostly glossy black, but a thin white stripe runs from the nose to the back of the forehead and a broad white stripe runs from the crown of the head over the nape, branching at the shoulders and along the upper sides, to the rump or onto the tip of the tail. Each front leg may also have a white stripe on the outside. The amount of white varies greatly from skunk to skunk. Cream-colored, brown, all-black, silvered and albino skunks have been reported.

Skunks molt in April, completing the process in September.

Males are larger than females. Adults are from 21.3 to 26.4 inches long, with a tail 7.1 to 11.4 inches and the hind foot 2.4 to 3.1 inches. They weigh 2.5 to 7.5 pounds.

Distribution: The striped skunk is found throughout southern Canada and the United States, except in arid areas of the southwest and in extreme northern Mexico.

Ecology: Skunks are found from sea level to timberline and live in a wide variety of habitats from brushy woods to quite large towns. They may dig their own burrows but prefer to use natural cavities among rocks, caves, under stone walls, logs and stumps. Mostly skunks use the abandoned burrows of woodchucks, red foxes, muskrats and others mammals. Most burrows are 6 to 20 feet long but may be as long as 50 feet. Burrows are generally 3 to

4 feet underground and end in one to three round chambers 12 to 15 inches in diameter. The chambers may be lined with leaves and grass. In cold weather the entrances are plugged. A den may have up to five well-hidden entrances.

Man, lynx, bobcats, foxes, coyotes and great horned owls prey on skunks. Most dogs avoid them after the first encounter. Many are killed by automobiles. They have fleas, ticks, lice and internal parasites. They are subject to a number of diseases, including distemper and rabies.

Behavior: Contrary to popular belief, skunk spray will not cause permanent damage to the eyes, but it does cause intense pain. The pungent fluid is composed of butylmercaptan, a sulphur-alcohol compound. The spray is a skunk's defense. When provoked, a skunk will arch its back, raise the tail high, stamp its front feet rapidly and shuffle backwards. Another misconception is that skunks can't spray while being held by the tail. They can.

Striped skunks are not social animals, but several may den together in winter. They are not agile and walk slowly. They don't climb trees and usually avoid water, but they can swim. They have only moderate abilities to see, hear and smell, but have a highly developed sense of touch. Usually silent, they growl, grunt, churr, squeal, chatter and hiss.

Skunks aren't wanderers. They will go about a half mile at night, although males in breeding season may travel 5 miles a night. Skunks are night animals; they are also active at dawn and dusk. Skunks seen about in broad daylight may be rabid. During late summer, striped skunks acquire a lot of body fat. They do not hibernate but go into a deep winter sleep.

They eat a great variety of insects, earthworms, snails, grains, nuts, corn, grasses, leaves, buds, apples, berries, bird eggs, frogs, snakes, turtles and their eggs, mice, voles, moles, shrews, rats, chipmunks, bats, squirrels, rabbits, garbage and carrion.

Striped skunks are polygamous. The breeding season starts in February and lasts to late March. Gestation lasts 62 to 68 days, and the kits are born in late April to early June, two to ten to the litter. They are thinly-furred, wrinkled and blind at birth. Their eyes open at 3 to 4 weeks old, and they are weaned at 6 to 8 weeks. About the time their eyes are open they can spray a small amount of fluid. They live to less than 4 years in the wild.

RIVER OTTER

River Otter
Lutra canadensis

River otters are playful. They enjoy tumbling, wrestling, chasing each other, following the leader and playing with rocks. They take delight in sliding down banks on their chests and bellies with their feet folded out of the way. The slide might be on steep grass, mud or snow-covered slopes, and may end in water or a snowdrift.

Description: The river otter is a streamlined animal that spends much of its time in the water. It has a long, round, muscular body and short, stout legs. The head is small and broad. The muzzle is short and the nose pad prominent and flat. The ears are short, and the small eyes are set high and forward on the head. The tail is long and round, thick at the base, tapering to a point. The feet have five webbed toes with strong claws. The coat is dense and sleek, composed of short, oily underfur mixed with long, glistening guard hairs. The ears and nose can be closed underwater.

Males and females look alike. They are a dark, rich brown in color, becoming somewhat paler or grayer below. The muzzle and throat are grayish. Black, slate, white and albino river otters rarely occur.

Males are slightly larger than females. Adults are from 35.1 to 51.2 inches long, with the tail 11.8 to 19.7 inches long and the hind foot 4.3 to 5.9 inches. They weigh 12 to 20 pounds, with some up to 30 pounds.

Distribution: The river otter is found throughout most of Canada and Alaska and the continental United States, except for in treeless and arid areas.

Ecology: River otters live along streams, sloughs, swamps, rivers and lakes. The well-hidden den may be merely a resting place beneath large roots, fallen trees, rocky ledges, in hollow logs, or in thickets near water. They may use an abandoned beaver lodge, muskrat house or woodchuck burrow. Dens along a stream or lake have an opening above water in summer and usually below the ice line in winter. River otters make both short and long tunnels. The floor of the den may be bare or covered with vegetation.

Man is their chief predator. Coyotes, lynx, foxes, bobcats and great horned owls may catch the young. They have ticks and internal parasites.

Behavior: Active year-round, otters are mostly night animals. They are intelligent, shy, gregarious and loyal to each other. They are strong and can whip a dog of the same size. They make low chuckles, chirps, purring grunts, growls, shrills, hissing barks and screams. Females caterwaul when mating.

Otters are excellent and graceful swimmers. Normally they swim by paddling with the hind feet, but when pressed they swim by writhing their bodies and tails. They may remain underwater for 2 minutes and swim to speeds of 7 miles an hour. They have been caught in nets as deep as 60 feet.

River otters are not fast runners and can lope or canter to 18 miles an hour. They are great travelers, known to go 100 miles or more seeking new territory. In summer otters remain close to water but in winter they may travel miles overland looking for places to get into the water and fish. They love to roll in the water and on land.

River otters feed on fish, crayfish, frogs, clams, salamanders, snails, turtles, earthworms, small snakes, birds and some plants. They may work together to herd fish into a cove to trap them. They eat fish on land, and may play with their catch before eating it piecemeal. They grub for aquatic animals by standing on their heads while rooting in mud and bottom debris, with only the tip of the tail showing at the water surface.

They are docile most of the year except in breeding season, when several males may follow a female and fight over her. Wild otters are thought to mate only in water. Breeding is thought to take place in March and April, and birth follows in 10 to 12 months due to delayed implantation of the fertilized egg in the womb. The litter has one to five kits, rarely six. The newborn are blind and toothless, with ears closed but fully furred. Their eyes open at about 35 days. The female does not allow the male near the kits until they leave the nest at about 10 to 12 weeks. They are weaned at 4 months but remain with their parents until about 1 year old. River otters live to 8 to 10 years in the wild.

Wild Cats

Members of the cat family, the Felidae, have specialized teeth for stabbing, slashing, and biting. The incisors are small and chisel-like; the canines are long, pointed, and slightly curved back.

Cats are efficient hunters that steathily stalk prey or lie in quiet ambush. They are agile climbers and good swimmers.

Cats are found worldwide except for in Antarctica and on remote ocean islands.

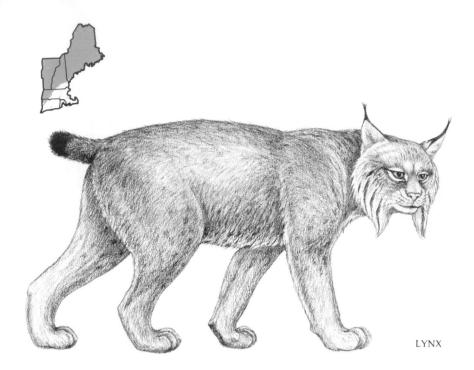

LYNX

Lynx
Lynx canadensis

The lynx is one of the rarest animals in New England, and, what with its preference for northern forests and night hunting, combined with its secretive habits, it is seldom observed.

Description: The lynx is stout-bodied and lean, twice as large as a domestic tomcat, with long, muscular legs, large, wide feet, a short, blunt tail with a completely black tip, and long, triangular, tufted ears. The head is short, low and broad.

The winter coat is long, thick, silky and loose, giving the lynx a fluffy look. Males and females look alike and color varies between animals. In winter the back is pale grizzled gray or brown. The guard hairs are white at the base, darkest in the middle and black at the tip. The crown of the head is brownish but has a lot of white-tipped hairs. The nose and cheeks are grayish. The insides of the ears are grayish-white and edged with buff; the outsides are black with a gray spot. The tips of the ear tufts and lines down the margins of the ears are brownish black. There are black spots at the corners of the mouth. The eyelids are white. The cheek ruffs, chin and throat are grayish white or light buffy brown mixed with brownish black bars. The underparts are buffy white, sparsely mottled with light brown. In winter the feet are heavily furred, top and bottom. The summer fur is darker, more grizzled and brownish.

The single molt annually begins in late spring and lasts to late fall. Albino and black lynx are rare.

Males are larger than females. They range from 32.7 to 39.4 inches long, with a tail 3.9 to 5.1 inches long and the hind foot 8.7 to 9.9 inches. They weigh 15 to 35 pounds.

Distribution: The original range was wooded North America south of the timberline from Alaska to Nova Scotia; south to southern New England and New York; west to the Michigan Upper Peninsula, northern Wisconsin, and southern Saskatchewan to the Pacific Ocean; and south through the Rockies into Colorado and central mountains of Utah. It has been eliminated from much of that range, and is rare in New England.

Ecology: Lynx live in deep, dark, unbroken forests. They rarely venture into open land. They den in a hollow tree, in tangled thickets, under logs, stumps, windfalls, or in rocky holes.

Man is their chief predator. Lynxes have fleas and internal parasites.

Behavior: They are active all year, mainly at night. They are mostly solitary animals.

Usually silent, lynx can purr, hiss, growl, spit, yowl, caterwaul, howl and mew. They are agile climbers and travel easily among fallen timber, moss-covered logs and boulders. They are slow on the ground and run with an awkward long gallop. A dog could easily outrun one. Lynx are good jumpers and swim well. They are powerful fighters. Inquisitive, they may follow a person for hours, but are not known to attack a man.

Lynx may hunt alone or in family groups spread out in a line across the woods. Population cycles for lynx seem closely related to the abundance of the snow shoe hare, their primary food in winter.

Besides snowshoe hares, lynx eat rabbits, squirrels, chipmunks, mice, skunks, porcupines, waterfowl, birds and their eggs, and occasionally fish and dead animals. Mature lynx have been known to kill young lynx.

Breeding takes place in late winter. Gestation is about 60 days, with one to four kittens in a litter. They are born in a natural cavity, on a ledge, or in a thicket. Their eyes open in 9 to 10 days, and they are weaned at 2 months. The family disbands in 6 to 9 months. They live 10 to 20 years.

Bobcat
Lynx rufus

Quick and strong, bobcats are strong fighters. A large bobcat can pull down and kill a deer.

Description: Bobcats differ from the lynx in having shorter legs, smaller feet with no hair on the bottoms, ears only slightly tufted, a longer tail that does not have black all the way around the tip, and shorter, more spotted fur.

The coat is dense, short and very soft when in prime condition. Males and females look alike. Color varies greatly from one bobcat to the next. In summer the back is grayish buff or reddish, spotted or streaked with black, darkest along the back from the head to the base of the tail, becoming lighter on the sides. The rump and hind legs are buff. The underparts are whitish with black spots, and there are black bars on the front legs. The head is streaked with black, and the buff neck is heavily spotted or streaked with black. The back of the ears are black and, when present, the small tufts are black. The eyelids are white. The tail has three or four distinct black bars. The bottom of the tail is whitish. Albino and black bobcats are rare. Molting begins in late summer.

Males are somewhat bigger than females. Adults are 28 to 47.3 inches long, with a tail 3.5 to 7.9 inches and a hind foot 6 to 8.7 inches. They weigh 15 to 45 pounds.

Distribution: Bobcats are found across southern Canada southward through the United States into most of Mexico.

Ecology: Bobcats roam wild, broken mountainous country with rocky, brushy cover. They frequently haunt spruce thickets and cedar swamps. In warm weather they hide in windfalls, under shrubs or low trees, or in rock crevices. They may den in rock crevices, under ledges, in caves, tree hollows, stumps or logs. The den is lined with dried grass, leaves, moss and other soft vegetation.

Man and dogs are their chief predators. A great horned owl may sometimes catch a young bobcat. They have fleas, ticks, lice and internal parasites. They get mange, rabies and feline enteritis.

Behavior: Solitary and elusive, bobcats are active year-round, mostly at night. They have a good sense of smell but rely mainly on their keen eyesight and hearing. When hunting they creep stealthily along from cover to cover until close enough to pounce, or they may lie motionless in a tree listening and watching for prey, or crouch in ambush on a trail. They will take to trees to rest, escape dogs, chase prey or catch birds.

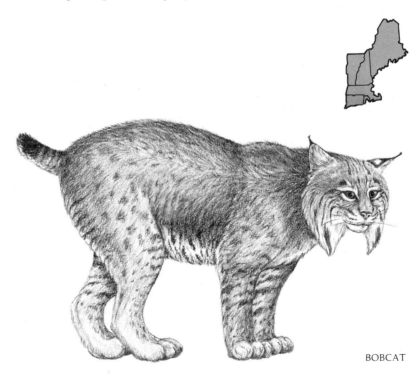

BOBCAT

They usually walk or trot but are not fast runners, hitting 15 miles an hour at best. They will go out of their way to avoid water but swim well.

Bobcats are quiet but can caterwaul, snarl, and spit with bared teeth at an enemy. They scream from time to time in breeding season.

The home range of a bobcat varies greatly with the abundance of food. One researcher said that their home range is rarely more than 2 square miles.

Deer and snowshoe hares are their main prey but they eat mice, squirrels, porcupines, mink, opossums, rabbits, skunks, muskrats, moles, shrews, chipmunks, birds and their eggs, fish, insects, dead animals and some plants.

Breeding season begins in late February and extends into March, although some females may breed as late as June. Gestation is about 62 days, with litters of one to four kittens. They are born blind and helpless. The eyes open at about 10 days, and kittens are weaned between 60 and 70 days.

8. Wing-footed Mammals

THE WALRUSES, SEALS, AND SEA LIONS are in a group of animals called Pinnipedia, Latin for "wing-footed," because their front and hind legs have been greatly modified into the form of flippers for swimming. These animals are adapted for life both on land and in the water. The body form is streamlined; their external ears are small or absent. The five fingers of each leg are covered with thick skin. The skin on the body is thick and tough, and they have large layers of blubber to provide insulation, buoyancy in water, padding, and reserve energy when food is scarce.

Pinnipeds are social animals, congregating on breeding grounds in large colonies called rookeries. Some spend up to 8 months at sea, while other species remain on land much of the time.

They are found along most shores and ice packs of the world, and in some rivers. A few have been isolated in lakes. Most species are found in polar and temperate waters, except the monk seals, which inhabit warm waters.

Hair Seals

Members of this family are also known as earless seals and are known scientifically as Phocidae. Besides having no external ears, they cannot turn their hind flippers forward along their body. On land they move like an inchworm, hunching forward, or rolling over sideways. The fur is stiff, with no woolly underfur.

Harbor Seal
Phoca vitulina concolor

Harbor seals have a strong liking for fresh water. They ascend rivers and enter lakes, sometimes far from the sea. Some live in lakes year round where open water is available.

Description: The harbor seal has a short, blunt, doglike muzzle with v-shaped nostrils, large eyes, a short neck and hairy flippers. The skull is thick with a large, deep lower jaw.
   Males and females look alike, but the color pattern is variable. They are essentially dark yellow-gray, mottled with irregular dark brown or black spots and a whitish network of broken small rings and loops above, paler below. When dry the coat

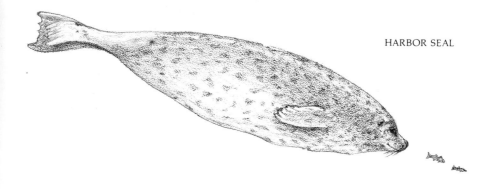

HARBOR SEAL

looks silvery.

Males are slightly larger than females. Adults are from 4 to 6 feet long and weigh 100 to 300 pounds.

Distribution: Harbor seals are widely distributed along coasts of oceans in the northern hemisphere. They are found in the western Atlantic, on both coasts of Greenland, and Ellesmere Island 79 °N, and south to Florida, but are more common from southern Greenland to Maine. In the past a few have found their way into Lake Champlain in Vermont.

Ecology: Harbor seals live mainly in coastal waters, harbors, bays, estuaries and rivers, and haul out on islands, mudbanks, sandbanks, rocky shores and ice.

Man, killer whales, polar bears and sharks prey on harbor seals. They have lice and internal parasites and can get a variety of diseases.

Behavior: Harbor seals are not migratory in general but will move because of heavy ice or lack of food. They form loosely organized colonies. Adults are active at high tide hours and generally haul out to rest and sleep at low tide, day or night. They are shy but curious and may gather around to look at a boat.

Adults make loud snorts, growls, barks, and grunts. Pups make bleats or mewing cries when lost. In water they play, roll, leap and swim in circles. They can swim to 13 knots and stay underwater for up to 15 minutes. On land they move slowly and with difficulty.

Harbor seals eat a wide variety of fish, shrimp, squids, and shelled animals.

They do not form harems but males do fight over females. Breeding takes place in the water in August. After a delay of the fertilized egg's implantation in the uterus, true gestation starts in October and lasts 7½ months. Pups are born later farther north, from late March through mid-June. At birth the pups weigh about 24 pounds and are immediately able to swim. They are nursed for 3 to 4 weeks. Harbor seals may live to 35 years.

Harp Seal
Pagophilus groenlandicus

For at least half the year the harp seal keeps close to the edge of drift ice in the North Atlantic.

Description: Harp seals get their name from a deep brown harp-shaped band or saddle that crosses the back along the shoulders and runs along the flank to near the tail in adult males. In females the band may be broken, indistinct or absent. Both sexes have a dark brown or blackish head to just behind the eye; the coloring of females is lighter or broken in spots. Newborn pups have long, silky, white fur which they shed in about a week. The nostrils are long and narrow. The baby fur is replaced in 3 to 4 weeks by a shorter silvery fur with brown spots. As the male matures the spots grow larger and darker, forming the saddle. Females may retain the spotted coat for some years.

Adults are about 6 feet long and weigh 400 pounds.

Distribution: Harp seals are found from the arctic coast of Russia to Greenland and on the northern coasts of Canada and Newfoundland. Stragglers have been reported as far south as Cape Henry, Virginia.

Ecology: Harp seals haul out on ice to molt and breed. Man is their chief predator. They have lice and internal parasites, and suffer from several diseases.

Behavior: Harp seals are gregarious and migratory; the herd moves south in winter when ice closes their feeding grounds and heads back north in spring when the pups leave the ice for the sea.

Harp seals feed mainly on capelin, a small fish, and various small crustaceans. They can swim up to 17 knots and remain submerged for about 20 minutes. They can dive to depths of 100 fathoms or more.

Harp seals appear to be promiscuous. In the northwestern Atlantic they breed in mid to late March. Implantation of the fertilized egg in the uterus is delayed about three months. Gestation takes about 12 months. At birth pups weigh about 15 pounds. They are weaned in 10 to 12 days and are independent of

the females in 2 weeks. Harp seals live about 20 years.

Gray Seal
Halichoerus grypus

As many as 100 gray seals occur in Maine waters, mainly in the approaches to Swans Island and Mount Desert Island and lower Penobscot Bay. A colony of about 15 lives at Nantucket Island, south of Cape Cod, Massachusetts.

Description: The gray seal has a straight and rather long head profile. Adult males have several conspicuous wrinkles on the stout neck. The muzzle is broad and donkey-like. The nostrils look like a "W" when seen from the front.

Male and female gray seals have considerable color variation. Some are all gray, others are blotched with irregular dark spots. They have dark backs and paler bellies.

Males are larger than females. Adult males are from 6 to 10 feet long and weigh 353 to 640 pounds. Females are 5.6 to 7.5 feet long and weigh 265 to 551 pounds.

Distribution: Gray seals are found on both sides of the North Atlantic and adjacent seas, with major populations in northwestern Europe, Iceland and eastern Canada. Some individuals stray as far south as New Jersey.

Ecology   Man is the main predator of gray seals. They have lice and internal parasites. Adults sometimes are infested with a green algae. Pups are susceptible to pneumonia.

Behavior: Gray seals usually haul out on secluded rock ledges. They are wary and spend much time in the water. They are ungainly on land, and waddle along on their chests. They are gregarious, living in loose colonies. They sleep underwater, on the surface and on land.

They disperse from the rookeries at the end of the breeding season, some pups going 600 miles from the place they were born.

Gray seals feed on a variety of fishes and on crustaceans, mollusks and squid.

In eastern Canadian waters the breeding season begins in late December when mature bulls and pregnant cows gather on reefs and islands. In early January the first breeders haul out on the islands to establish territories. Established bulls are often challenged, and fighting occurs. Gray seals are polygamous; a male will keep a harem of up to six breeding cows. Pupping occurs from late December through mid-February. The newborn pups are 35 inches long and weigh about 30 pounds. They are weaned at 3 weeks but remain ashore for at least a month. They live to about 40 years in the wild.

GRAY SEAL

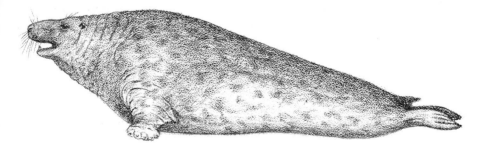

HOODED SEAL

Hooded Seal
Cystophora cristata

The most remarkable feature of this seal is the enlarged skin of the snout which forms a hood on top of the head from the snout to just past level of the eyes in the males.

Description: The hood becomes progressively larger as the seal grows older. It is covered with short, stiff, black hairs and is about 12 inches long and 7 inches in diameter when inflated. When the hood is deflated it hangs down loosely in front of the mouth. The hood may be inflated when the seal is calm, excited, or angry. In addition to the hood, the males have an inflatable nasal sac which can be blown out through the nostrils like a red balloon. The balloon is extruded through one nostril while the other is kept shut. It is about 6 inches long and 6 inches wide and can be drawn in and out several times in quick succession as the male shakes its head up and down. It is not inflated while the hood is inflated.

Adults are slate blue or brownish above, with a pattern of irregular dark spots on the back that shade to silver gray on the sides and belly. The muzzle and face of males are blackish. The faces of females and young are blackish to just behind the eyes. At birth the pups have a lustrous fur, bluish black above and silvery white below.

Males are larger than females. They measure 7 to 11 feet long and weigh about 900 pounds. Females are up to 10 feet long and weigh about 600 pounds.

Distribution: Hooded seals are associated with the ice pack in deep waters of the Arctic and Atlantic Oceans from northern Siberia and Barents Sea to Jan Mayen Island, Iceland; Denmark Strait, southern Greenland; Baffin Island, Newfoundland; and the Gulf of St. Lawrence. Only strays are found in New England waters.

Ecology: Hooded seals haul out on large, heavy floes of arctic ice to molt and reproduce. Man and polar bears are their main predators. They have lice and internal parasites.

Behavior: Hooded seals are rather quarrelsome and much less gregarious than harp seals. They are solitary except during the molting and breeding seasons. Adults fiercely defend their pups. They are nomadic and prefer thick ice floes on the high seas, rarely hauling out on land. They swim slowly, with the top of the head just above the water.

Hooded seals usually form family groups consisting of the bull, the cow and their pup. Sometimes they stay a considerable distance from the nearest breathing hole or open water. They eat fish, squid, shrimp, octopus and mussels.

Pups are born on the ice in late February to late March. They are about 3.6 feet long and weigh 24 to 33 pounds. They are nursed 3 to 4 weeks. During this time the bulls remain nearby, and just after weaning the adults breed and return to sea. The pups remain on the ice for the first 20 to 22 days of life and then disperse at sea.

9. Hoofed Mammals

THE HOOFED ANIMALS are in the Artiodactyla order. They all have specialized feet in which the body weight is carried on the third and fourth toes, which are formed into hard hoofs. They have an even number of toes, as opposed to the Perissodctyla, an order characterized by an odd number of toes, which includes horses, tapirs, and the rhinoceros.

Most of the mammals in this group are plant eaters and browse or graze. Most also chew a cud.

They occur worldwide as native wild animals except in Australia, Antarctica and unpopulated islands. They include such diverse animals as hippopotamuses, camels, giraffes, deer, sheep, cattle, peccaries, pronghorn antelopes and bison.

Deer

Members of the deer family, or *Cervidae*, are known by their paired antlers, primarily in the males, but in both sexes in caribou. Antlers are absent in musk deer and Chinese water deer. Deer have no upper incisor teeth, and some species have no upper canine teeth.

Antlers are not bones but bone-like structures that are shed each season. They begin to grow in the spring with swelling of buds from a bony area on the top of the head. During the fastest growing time, the antlers are soft and tender and covered with soft, hairy skin, richly supplied with blood vessels which carry nutrients to the growing antlers.

By early fall the antlers reach full development, and the blood vessels shut off and the velvety skin begins to dry up and peel. The dried velvet is rubbed off against trees, shrubs and rocks. By late winter the antlers begin to loosen and fall one at a time.

White-tailed Deer

Odocoileus virginianus borealis

Antlers are formidable weapons among fighting bucks during breeding season, and captive bucks have been known to use them against humans. At times the antlers of two fighting bucks become entangled, and the deer slowly succumb to starvation.

Description: The graceful white-tailed deer has long legs, large ears, a long, bushy tail, a black nose pad, and narrow hooves. The males have antlers.

The sexes are alike in coloring. The summer coat is reddish and the winter coat grayish. The coat is short, thin, straight and somewhat wiry in summer. The winter coat is long and thick, and may be slightly crinkled. The hair is hollow.

In summer the back is reddish brown to tan, sometimes paler on the sides. The underparts and insides of the legs are white. The top of the head and the tip of the ears are often tipped with reddish tawny hairs. There is a white.patch on the throat and white across the blackish nose, around the eyes and inside the ears. There is a black spot on either side of the white chin. The

WHITE-TAILED DEER

tail is dusky above and white around the edges and below. When the deer runs, it raises its tail to show a white "flag." In winter the upper fur is grayish brown or grayish.

Fawns are reddish brown with white spots on the back. They begin to lose their white spots at 3 to 4 months old.

Deer have a fall molt from August to mid-September and a spring molt that begins in May or June. Albino and blackish deer are rare.

The males have moderately spreading, large, branching antlers. The main beams grow slightly outward and back at first, then directly forward and slightly inward. Each beam bears several tines that appear to grow vertically.

Deer antlers are shed annually, usually from mid-December to mid-January. They begin to grow in April or May and become hard by September when the velvet dries up. The color varies from white to deep brown.

While the size and number of tines on deer antlers are not

determined solely by age, older deer tend to have larger antlers with more points. In young bucks, especially yearlings, the antlers do not develop tines. Such deer with single tines are called spikehorns. The quality of available food and heredity both affect antler growth. Occasionally does have antlers, and a 210-pound doe shot in Maine in 1980 had antlers with 8 points.

Bucks are larger than does. Adult bucks average 71 inches long, with a tail 11 inches long, and stand 39 inches at the shoulder. The average field-dressed (without internal organs) weight of buck deer is 122 pounds. In 1979 two bucks shot in Maine weighed 277 pounds, field-dressed. Such large bucks would weigh well in excess of 300 pounds, live weight. Does weigh an average of 93 pounds, field-dressed.

Distribution: They are found over most of southern Canada, the United States (except for most of California, Nevada and Utah), and south to Coiba Island, Panama.

Ecology: The white-tailed deer is a forest edge animal, preferring thickets alternating with open, sunny glades and abandoned fields. During early summer, the deer feed near and in lakes, ponds, and streams where there are abundant grasses, pond weeds, and other succulent plants.

White-tailed deer will bed down in a little hollow where the ground is level, grassy or dry. Bedding spots may be found in hardwood habitats and in tall meadow grasses with a vantage point. They may use a bed only once or repeatedly.

During most of the year, deer are.widely distributed wherever there is cover and food. During severe winter weather they "yard up" in a network of trails packed into deep snow. Dense stands of mature trees are favored for yarding, usually with lots of evergreens.

Man and dog are the chief predators of deer. Coyotes and bobcats also kill them. Deer have lice, ticks, mites, and a variety of internal parasites. They are subjects to a wide variety of diseases.

Behavior: White-tailed deer are cautious and alert. They are also curious. Their eyesight is good for detecting moving objects, but they do not seem as able to detect stationary objects. They have keen senses of smell and hearing. They seem able to detect the slightest sound or unnatural odor in their area.

They make bleats, whistles, whines, loud snorts, squawks and "whiews." The doe gives a low whining sound to call her fawns. Fawns bleat.

They normally walk or trot at a leisurely pace, but can run up to 25 miles an hour and are excellent bounders and jumpers. They are very strong swimmers and readily take to the water to reach new feeding areas or to escape pursuit.

White-tailed deer are somewhat social, living in loosely organized family groups after the rutting season. Deer activity depends on local conditions, season, weather conditions and individual natures. In areas where they are hunted they keep to their beds during the better part of the day, feeding mostly at night. Normally they feed from dawn to a few hours later, then wander a brushy hillside or to a ridgetop to lie down for the afternoon,.feeding again from dusk to dawn.

They follow much the same routine day after day, establishing well-trodden deer trails. In moving about they tend to take the path of least resistance. They may remain within an area of 2 to 3 square miles for weeks.

Deer are mostly browsers, but graze occasionally on grasses, lichens, mushrooms and other non-woody plants. The variety of foods eaten by white-tailed deer is enormous and covers almost any plant growth found in their range.

The rutting urge develops earlier in bucks than in does. In northern woods from late September through mid-November the bucks' necks swell, and they begin to spar with bushes and small trees. Bucks move about extensively during the rut, mating with every receptive doe they find. Two or more bucks may follow and fight, sometimes savagely, over the same doe.

Gestation lasts about 200 days. The number of fawns varies one to four, averaging two fawns per doe; the number is affected by the condition of the mother, well-fed does producing more fawns.

At birthing time, the doe seeks a secluded spot. Birth is usually quick once labor starts. The newborn fawn is weak and wobbly and remains hidden in cover; it will instinctively flatten against the ground and remain still when danger threatens. Fawns vary from 3 to almost 15 pounds at birth, and will stand in about 12 hours. They begin to nibble on greens at 2 to 3 weeks old, and they are weaned at about 4 months. During their first summer the fawns follow their mother closely. Captive white-tailed deer have lived up to 20 years.

Moose
Alces alces americana

The ungainly moose is the largest of all the deer family. Mature bulls reach 1,400 pounds in New England.

Description: Moose have long legs, a short neck, very short tail, a high hump on the shoulders, and a small rump. There is a slight mane on the neck and shoulders.

The head is large but narrow, with large ears and small eyes. The muzzle is broad, inflated and pendulous, with the front end of the upper lip overhanging the lower.

Males and females have a dewlap of skin and hair called a "bell" that hangs from the underside of the throat. It is large in males, but its function is unknown.

The front legs are longer than the hind legs. This makes the gait awkward but helps in jumping over fallen trees. The hooves are long, narrow and pointed.

Adult males have massive antlers, broadly palmated (lobed) with many tines. New antlers start to grow in April, slowly at first, but rapidly as summer advances. They are fully developed by August or September, when the velvet is dried and is scraped off on bushes and trees. Antlers are usually shed in December or January.

The fur is very thick and brittle, about 6 inches long on the neck and shoulders. Males and females are colored alike. The new spring coat is blackish brown and grayish brown, paler on the head and sometimes gray on the face. The underparts are the same color except that the lower belly and lower legs are lighter or pale brownish gray. The summer coat is lighter. The calf is reddish brown.

The annual molt takes place in spring.

Females average three quarters the size of males. Adults average 114 inches long, and stand 72 inches high at the shoulder. The tail is about 2 inches long. Antlers average 58 inches wide.

Distribution: Moose are found well below timberline and on the tundra between the Alaska-Yukon boundary and Hudson Bay, and in parts of the northern United States. They are found in New England south to Pennsylvania, westward across southern Ontario and northern Wisconsin and Minnesota to the Rocky

Mountains, with a southern extension into Wyoming and northeastern Utah. The present range is much reduced. The eastern moose is found in eastern Canada, from Nova Scotia and New Brunswick west through Quebec to eastern Ontario, south into Maine, northern New Hampshire and Vermont. Some stragglers make it into Massachusetts and Connecticut.

Ecology: Moose inhabit northern forests, thickets, swamps and swales that provide plants to eat and good cover. In summer they frequent streams, ponds and shallow lakes, both to eat water plants and to evade biting insects.

Man is the chief moose predator. Bears may kill calves. Parasites include ticks, mooseflies, blackflies, and internal parasites. They have a number of diseases.

Behavior: Moose are very alert. They have keen smell and vision but poor eyesight. They are not very social, but during

MOOSE

summer several may congregate in a large body of shallow water to eat water plants. They may lie in shallow water to escape flies. When snow is deep, as many as 15 moose may yard together.

Moose are most active at dawn and dusk. They will lie up in dense forest cover in foggy, rainy or windy weather when they have difficulty hearing or picking up scent. They normally stay in an area with a radius of 2 to 10 miles if food is adequate. They move around more extensively in breeding season, and a bull may respond to a cow's bellow from 2 miles away.

Moose walk casually, trot gracefully or gallop clumsily. They can be heard moving through brush from several yards away when undisturbed. They move silently when alerted but will crash noisily through branches when frightened. They can run up to 35 miles an hour. Moose can walk easily through deep bogs. They are strong swimmers.

Moose are silent, except during breeding season, and except for cows with calves. The bull utters either a low, moo-like plea, broken off short with an upward inflection at the end, or a throaty gulp. The cow's call is longer and more like that of a domestic cow, but not as loud. The moose calf sounds like a domestic calf. Cows call to calves with a grunt.

Moose are mainly browsers but sometimes graze on grass, moss, lichens, mushrooms and leafy plants. They eat a wide variety of plants. Because of their short necks, moose commonly are forced to bend, spread their front legs, or drop on their knees to feed from the ground. They often rear up on their hind legs to reach tree twigs, and they may straddle and ride down small saplings by walking over them to get at the twigs.

The food moose eat generally has a low nutritional value so they eat large amounts, estimated at 35 pounds a day for a 1,200-pound moose.

By early to mid-September the rut becomes established. Large bulls show interest in the cows and force young bulls to keep their distance, and they will investigate any low, blatting call of a cow.

Bulls paw out depressions or wallows in damp ground and urinate in them. A wallow in use has a musky odor. The exact function of the wallows is not known, but it may be related to the rut. The breeding season extends through October, bulls generally staying with one cow at a time for 7 to 12 days then leaving to find another mate. Serious fights may occur between bulls during the breeding season, and they lock antlers at times.

Gestation is 240 to 246 days. There are one or two calves per litter. Triplets are rare. At birth the calves weigh 25 to 35 pounds and they grow rapidly, gaining 1 to 2 pounds a day during the first month. The newborn moose is awkward and helpless. It is often kept hidden by the cow. One or two weeks before giving birth the cow will drive away her yearling calves.

The prime of life for a moose is between 6 and 10 years. These animals may live to 23 years.

Fallow Deer
Cervus dama

Fallow deer were released on Nantucket Island and Martha's Vineyard, Massachusetts, during the 1930's. They occur as wild animals on Martha's Vineyard now.

Description: From May to October, male and female fallow deer may be various shades of bright fawn or yellowish brown on the head and neck, and dappled with white, or yellowish white, spots on the back and flanks. The throat, underparts, insides of the legs, bottom of the tail and the rump are whitish. A black line runs down the middle of the back from the nape to the end of the tail. There is often a white line separating the upper and lower colors. In winter the coat becomes darker and the spots less distinct.

There is considerable variation in color on fallow deer. At times the entire summer coat may be a uniform glossy brown, without spots, and sooty gray below. Other color variations include white, albino, black, and bluish. Fawns are slightly darker than adults and may not be spotted.

In adult males the antlers are shaped somewhat like those of a moose, flattened and broadly lobed, with many tines. The velvet is usually shed in late August or September. As with other deer, antler growth is closely associated with quality of habitat.

Males are larger than females. They are 51 to 63 inches long, with a tail 6.7 to 9.1 inches, standing 32 to 36 inches at the shoulders. Adult females weigh 51 to 57 pounds and adult males 130 to 320 pounds.

FALLOW DEER

Distribution: Fallow deer are native to Asia Minor and countries bordering the Mediterranean Sea. They have been successfully introduced into central Europe. Fallow deer are prized for their beauty and are found in zoos, in parks, and on private estates all over the world.

Ecology: Man and dogs are their chief predators on Martha's Vineyard.

Behavior: Fallow deer have keen senses of smell and hearing and good eyesight. They are usually silent. Does and fawns utter low wickering noises, and does may make a plaintive cry to call a fawn and during the rut. When suspicious or curious they utter a short, deep bark. During the rut bucks belch and grunt.

Fallow deer are gregarious but the bucks remain apart from the does except during the breeding season and early winter. During summer they are most active in the morning and evening, but they feed all day in the winter. They move about quietly when feeding, walking at a steady pace and stopping often to look and listen. When they spot danger they raise the tail and take up to five bounds on stiff legs to warn other deer. They can jump high fences.

They browse on the twigs, shoots, leaves and bark of most hardwood trees and also eat a variety of grasses, herbs, berries, fruits, acorns and mushrooms.

10. Extirpated Mammals

THERE IS NOTHING NEW about mammals being eliminated from the New England landscape. Mammoths, mastodons, bisons and other mammals once roamed this area. But the arrival of the white man has directly contributed to the elimination of a number of mammals in more recent history. Among these animals are the eastern wolf, wolverine, eastern mountain lion, wapiti (elk) and caribou.

Eastern Timber Wolf
Canis lupus lycaon

The timber wolf greatly resembles a huge German shepherd dog and may reach a weight of 100 pounds. As early as 1631 the Plymouth and Massachusetts Bay colonies waged war on the wolves, which were considered a threat to livestock. Just when the last wolf in New England died is not clear from records. A wolf was reported killed in Addison County, Vermont, about 1830, but individual wolves were probably present in New England well after that time. Although still present in southern Quebec, Ontario, and parts of northern Minnesota and northern Michigan, the eastern timber wolf is an endangered species in the United States.

Wolverine
Gulo luscus luscus

The wolverine was never abundant in New England; it apparently has been found only in northern parts of Vermont and Maine and probably in the western highlands of Massachusetts. The wolverine is the largest member of the weasel family, weighing 24 ot 40 pounds. Wolverines are powerful, low-built, burly mammals, and one could be confused for a small bear from a distance, except for its long, bushy tail. They are solitary animals and are known for their willingness to fight much larger animals for food.

Eastern Mountain Lion
Felis Concolor couguar

Stories of mountain lion sightings and mountain lion tracks are continually reported in northern New England, but no mountain lions have been taken in the six states over the past 70 years. Next to the jaguar, the mountain lion is the largest native cat in

EASTERN TIMBER WOLF

WOLVERINE

EASTERN MOUNTAIN LION

North America. These animals reach weights exceeding 200 pounds. The mountain lion once had the widest distribution of any American mammal, and was at home in an extraordinary variety of conditions. Since 1900, this species has been extirpated east of the Mississippi River, except for a declining population in Florida and New Brunswick. The mountain lion still roams west of the 100th meridian in wilderness areas in most of the Rocky Mountain states.

Walrus
Odobenus rosmarus

Fossil walrus bones estimated to be upwards of 15,000 years old have been recorded as far south as Virginia. One animal was taken at Plymouth Bay, Massachusetts, in December 1734. The walrus is most easily identified by the long tusks which protrude from the upper jaw. The tusks may be as long as 25 inches and weigh 11 pounds in males. Male walruses are about a third bigger than females and reach weights of up to 2,000 pounds.

WALRUS

Extirpated Mammals

203

American Elk
Cervus elaphus

The Shawnee Indians called this animal "wapiti," but the early settlers called it an elk because it closely resembled the European red deer of that name. The wapiti is second only to the moose in weight among deer and is the handsomest member of the family with its immense antlers. Adult males average 700 pounds. Once the wapiti was the most widely distributed of the hoofed game animals, found in most of temperate North America from parts of Canada south to northern Mexico. Several times during the late 1800's and the 1900's wapiti have been introduced in New Hampshire, but there are no free-ranging elk now in New England.

Eastern Woodland Caribou
Rangifer tarandus caribou

The woodland caribou was once found in the northern forested borders from Alaska and Canada south to northern Maine, northern Minnesota, Idaho and British Columbia. It is nearly

extinct over much of its range. The last caribou sighting in Maine was reported in 1908. In 1963, twenty-four adult woodland caribou were introduced from the Newfoundland to Maine, near Mount Katahdin, but none of them were reported seen after 1967.

Sea Mink
Mustela vison macrodon

The probable distribution of the sea mink was along the North Atlantic seaboard to the coast of Connecticut. It is known only from skeletal remains that have been unearthed. A trader from Brewer, Maine (who traded for some 50,000 mink skins with Indians from the Penobscot and Jericho Bay region), is said to have claimed that the species became extinct about 1860. The fur of the sea mink was reported much coarser and more reddish than that of the common inland mink.

Index